THE ODDEST BOOK IN YOUR SHELF

FURLED

BLUEROSE PUBLISHERS
India | U.K.

Copyright © Furled 2024

All rights reserved by author. No part of this publication may be reproduced, stored in a retrieval system or transmitted in any form or by any means, electronic, mechanical, photocopying, recording or otherwise, without the prior permission of the author. Although every precaution has been taken to verify the accuracy of the information contained herein, the publisher assume no responsibility for any errors or omissions. No liability is assumed for damages that may result from the use of information contained within.

BlueRose Publishers takes no responsibility for any damages, losses, or liabilities that may arise from the use or misuse of the information, products, or services provided in this publication.

For permissions requests or inquiries regarding this publication, please contact:

BLUEROSE PUBLISHERS
www.BlueRoseONE.com
info@bluerosepublishers.com
+91 8882 898 898
+4407342408967

ISBN: 978-93-6261-572-5

First Edition: June 2024

FURLED
an attempt to unfurl

[Furl : neatly and securely rolled or folded up]

PREFACE

Hey there, delightful souls! I'm Furled, the whimsical mind behind the pages you hold. As I take a moment to introduce you to this collection, imagine us sharing a cup of coffee under the evening sky, where the sun and moon play tag.

Before we dive into this collection, I want to share a little story behind the radiant theme that colors these tales.

Picture a shopping spree with my siblings, each claiming their colors for our signature twin look. But, oh, there it was—the lonely yellow dress, abandoned like a forgotten melody. Feeling a pang of sympathy, I decided to rescue it from its retail exile. Little did I know, I was weaving my life into the hues of yellow.

Yellow transformed from an unnoticed hue to a magic wand, making me feel playful, whimsical, and as light as a feather caught in a sunlit breeze. It turned ordinary moments into a gleaming dance of joy.

So, in these tales, poems, and reflections, let the radiant yellow be your joy guide. It's not just a color; it's a burst of laughter, a sprinkle of fun, and the warmth that wraps around you like a cheerful hug.

Growing up is a bit like chasing sunsets, isn't it? In my late teens, I discovered the beauty in the fleeting moments, the magic in the mundane, and the joy in the dance of moonbeams.

Growing into adulthood unfolded like a series of sunsets and moonlit epiphanies, each page a testament to the gentle nudges of hope. It's my earnest desire that this book reflects the warmth of those moments.

As you immerse yourself, discover a collection crafted to bring a smile to your face and resonate with the beats of your own heart. Every word is a brushstroke painting a canvas of positivity, with the hope of Allah as the guiding light.

To you, my cherished reader, thank you for joining me on this expedition. My aim is simple: to illuminate your days with positivity, to be a companion in your journey, and to echo the whispers of hope that resonate beyond these pages.

Page after page, you'll find sunsets that spill joy, moonlit tales that whisper solace, and reflections that anchor in the hope of Allah. You'll find this book to be a kaleidoscope of poems, tales, and extracts from my diary. May each chapter be a step closer to the dawn you seek.

As we embark on this shared odyssey, may the positivity within these lines be a balm for your soul. May the yellow palette of joy bring a twinkle to your eyes, just as it did for me on that serendipitous day of shopping.

Here's to sunsets, moonlit skies, the unwavering hope that we carry within and the magic of turning twenty!

Furled

I've poured my soul onto these pages, crafting each word as a balm and a warm embrace for you, dear reader. Within this book lies a tapestry of emotions woven from my brightest days and darkest nights, and moments of tranquil reflection while strolling in my balcony gazing at pretty sunsets and on cool calming starry nights with sparkly moon beam. I extend my deepest gratitude to those whove shared in my dusk and witnessed my unfurling.

As you delve into these verses, may you find solace and companionship in the echoes of your own journey. For just as I've laid bare my heart, I invite you to unfurl yours too, and together, let us embrace the beauty of being truly alive. Let's together become unfurled butterflies, framed within the canvas of life.

In this book, there isn't a particular genre or theme; it's a compilation of all my writings from the past two years, now in book form, fulfilling my promise to my yellows. It's also a way to preserve them forever, so I can show them to my kids later on and perhaps tease them a bit—well, inspire them, too, of course, haha.

In the opening chapters, you'll find poetry and reflections on my evenings. Each chapter serves a different purpose, but they all share the intention of connecting with you and instilling hope in your hearts.

In the last chapter, something very dear to me, I've written about my parents and a few other things in Urdu.

PROLOGUE

In the hushed corridors of my thoughts, I invite you to wander through the labyrinth of my soul. This isn't merely a journal; it's a symphony of whispered confessions, ink-stained revelations, and the silent echoes of a journey untold.

Within these pages lie the fragments of my existence—poems birthed in the shadows, incidents etched in the margins, reflections scribbled in the margins of life's unfolding chapters. A collage of moments, a kaleidoscope of emotions.

As you embark upon this intimate odyssey, let the ink-stained quill be your guide, and the parchment, a canvas for the kaleidoscopic hues of my inner world. Each page is a mirror reflecting the dance between solitude and connection, chaos and serenity.

Reader, embrace the ambiguity, for in these scattered verses and prose, you'll find the mosaic of a life, unfiltered and unapologetically raw.

So, grab your popcorn (or your preferred snack; I'm not here to judge), and let's dive into the chaos, the confetti, and the downright confessions of a life lived with a touch of whimsy and a pinch of unpredictable hilarity.

**Emerging from your
chrysalis,
unfurl your wings and fly,
each graceful motion
painting hues of
happiness and beauty.
Amidst life's storms,
know your delicate wings
are strong enough to soar.
Trust in their beauty to
transform every storm into
something truly remarkable.**

                         - FURLED

ACKNOWLEDGEMENT

First and foremost, I want to express my heartfelt gratitude to the Almighty for being the ultimate GPS on this rollercoaster ride of writing, for it is through His guidance that I have found success on this journey.

We all experience that sudden spark, igniting within us in various forms, propelling us forward. Before embarking on this journey, I never imagined reaching this point. It was the influence of a random stranger, blessed with a beautiful heart and an extraordinary artistic mind, that became my sole motivation. To that person, whose identity remains unknown, I owe a debt of gratitude. Their inspiration led me to encounter countless remarkable individuals who have become the cherished companions of my life's voyage.

The reviews, feedback, and resonance from readers have been the driving force behind my continuous writing. Your praises, though sometimes more inflated than a bouncy castle, kept me soaring through doubt-filled clouds. Without your encouragement, this book might've ended up as nothing more than a collection of doodles in the margins of my notebooks.

Without them, I would not have traversed this far. Fulfilling my promise to compile my writings into a book was a commitment I once doubted. In moments of self-doubt, it was their encouragement that lifted me, affirming the beauty of my wings and urging me to soar higher. Their trust in my abilities has brought me to this juncture.

A special acknowledgment to my friends who dedicated their time and creativity to help me with the book covers. Despite their busy schedules, they produced covers that were truly beautiful, each one a testament to their talent. Although I ultimately chose to use my own cover for this book—a decision I'm still pondering—I am excited to feature their stunning work in my future publications. Thank you for your unwavering support and artistic contributions.

Finalizing the title proved to be a daunting task! They patiently helped me select a title, even when I asked so many times that it irritated them. In the end, I went with my own random title.

To my family and my friends, reading this, you must be surprised by this version of me. Perhaps you have stumbled upon my modest online presence, a journey I embarked on over few years ago. Never did I envision reaching this milestone. Initially, it served as a means to document my moments of joy, cringe, and sorrow. The reason for my secrecy lies in my inability to express myself fully in your presence, perhaps due to a sense of discomfort.

Thanks to my siblings for being my secret keepers and cheerleaders, even if Mom's dying to brag about my writing skills to the others. Sorry, Mom, your star author's still in incognito mode, but your pride is felt from miles away.

I am grateful to Allah for allowing my words to resonate with others' hearts, and I pray that they touch yours as well.

I extend my heartfelt gratitude to my publishers, who are turning my dream into reality. Who not only assisted me with this endeavor but also inspired me and instilled belief in myself.

I'm immensely grateful to all my friends who have stood by me, especially those eagerly awaiting to be the first buyer. Their unwavering support and belief in me have been truly uplifting. Though I can't list all their names, I deeply appreciate each one of them. Their encouragement and motivation have been invaluable, keeping me focused and determined. I pray for their well-being and success.

Lastly, I extend my heartfelt thanks to the readers who accompany me on this poetic odyssey. Your boundless enthusiasm paints the pages with vibrant hues, turning mere words into a symphony of shared dreams.

Butterflies, fragile and free,
Teach us patience, to let things be.
Impatience whispers, but we resist,
Trusting the process, we persist.

In life's dance, a rhythm unfolds,
Trusting ourselves, as the story molds.
With patience and faith, we'll ascend,
To reach our dreams, where journeys blend.

I draw them

CONTENT

Chapter 1 - Moonlit Episodes

Chapter 2 - Whirlwind of Words

Chapter 3 - Tiny Tales

Chapter 4 - Evening Musings

Chapter 5 - Inward Echoes

Chapter 6 - For Us

Chapter 7 - Homebound Narratives

Chapter 8 - A Pallete of Feelings

Chapter 9 - Jazbath - e - Urdu

Start with a radiant smile, and dive into the swinging adventure – relish the linguistic ride like basking in the tranquil joy of a gentle swing.

CH 01
MOONLIT
episodes

LOST IN THE COSMOS OF LOVE

This took me longer to realise,
that every night I go out,
I find myself in the maze of stars,
They do catch my eyes,
as they're many in number,
But that rare view of your sparkle
makes me catch my breath.
I wouldn't mind to be lost
forever in the universe,
if it's meant to search you.

If I find you~
my gazing eyes wouldn't blink,
when I actually get a chance
 to indulge myself
 <in you>

                                                to moon

WHISPERS OF THE NIGHT
Moonlit Yearnings

Be it a crescent, or a full you
I 'will' to be with you.

and on those cloudy nights,
when you stay hidden
for you, my heart longs even more.

but those tiny sparkles of you,
that reflects on the dark sky,
makes my ray of hope shine,
that I would get another chance
to indulge myself
 <in you> again

YOUR MOON

As you're still in my heart...
when i look at the moon,
it reminds me of our depart
as i was once your moon
which couldn't fit in your sky.
Don't let my fading affect you,
as I leave behind my shine
to reflect your smiling eyes ;
and my traces to make your heart
bloom and not leave it in gloom.
I'll fade peacefully,
as i left you in Allah's care.

DEAR MOON
A Poetic Reflection on Radiance in the Darkest Nights

"Even in your lowest days,
you still manage to radiate just as the moon does in the darkest nights.
Even though it cannot light the whole world, it still manages to make the clouds around it gleam like gold."

GALACTIC LOVE SYMPHONY

A Poetic Ode to Our Celestial Connection

I'm honoured to be your galaxy,
to be the ocean where,
you dive with your poetry.
All the pretty things hanging in the sky
reminds me of you.
I'm in awe with the way you interpret
everything into a romantic fantasy..
Just to let you know that,
I'm aware of your world,
and I bear witness for it
My heart race when I see
your words parading to
my soul, my world.
Sun melts and Moon withers
when compared with your love.

Your heart that radiates
as bright as a Quasar,
I want you to be aware of
how bright your star looks
from my world,
as you've always been
whirling around my universe.
And to kiss goodbye to your longingness
I would fly beyond the 7 skies
and dive into the deepest oceans
Only if it's meant to enter
your fantasy world.
So that we can be two bright stars
forming the best constellation
the world has ever witnessed to.

Quasars are amongst the most luminous
objects in the known Universe.

CH 02
WHIRLWIND OF WORDS *Poetic Storms Unleashed*

CHAOS BENEATH TRANQUILITY

A Reflection

I'm all chaos inside,
but seem like a silent sea,
with a silly smile to scumble
over my uncertainties;
Coating the empty shades
of blue and yellow
with a wave of tranquility;
Oh my perplexed self,
will your heart ever be
like a serene sea,
Just as you seem to be?

A SYMPHONY OF CHAOS
Unearthing the Beauty Within

When hearts filled with serenity,
unclouded, calm, and windless,
Blows with unforeseen waves,
waves of beautiful chaos,
Whirling the heap of emotions,
emotions which were deeply buried.

When the dimness of my heart was overshot
with these iridescent light,
light of sensations, feelings and emotions;
Began enhancement of windless wind
around the barren lands of my heart.

Surely, there's a certain beauty in chaos,
When sprinkled over the gaps of
my scattered heart,
Flowers sprouts out magnificently,
moulding my heart into a luxuriant shore.

EMBRACING SCARS

A Tapestry of Strength and Beauty

I hate scars
as they diminish my beauty,
worth, and confidence.
But to the people who truly love me,
they wouldn't bother.
They would ignore them as if
they've never seen them.

Yet, they're on a constant struggle,
deep in their hearts,
thinking of ways
to help me love my scars
and let them fade away
in a beautiful way.

But you've got to have them.
If you do, don't bother looking at them
with feelings of rage.
Just accept them
as a temporary part of you,
which will definitely heal someday.
Someday, In Shaa Allah.

And if you have scars which has
been with you forever,
and will be with you for eternity
Adorn yourself with it, and
walk gracefully with your head held high,
For there's no one as strong, as brave,
as beautiful as you, my love ♡

And if scars are covered,
in fear of judgement,
uncover them with love,
with kisses and warm hugs.
Embrace them elegantly,
for they are alluring, and
enhances your beauty.
They don't make you odd,
but makes you stand out prettily ♡
Pretily in the crowd of odds.

Scarred hearts are better.
Better than barren hearts.
For they can heal and bloom.
It's better than a seal
on barren heart,
where nothing flourish.

THE SUN WONDERS ABOUT THE MOON'S LOVE

Why is that when clouds cover me,
they raise with joy?
And when you get covered,
they sigh with despair?

Why is that they find you pleasant but not me,
when what we both do is light up the sky?

Why do they only write poetries on you
and not on me,
when I shone on their beautiful beginnings?

Why do they not see me enlightening their lives,
Instead search for it in your moonlight?

Why is that my light make their eyes shut and
yours let them dive deep into your eyes ?

a convo between sun and moon

Yeah I know, I sometimes become more harsh,
but does that mean, I'm unloved?
When you are still loved during all your phases?

Why do they rejoice while seeing you in a blue sky,
When I'm still up at the other corner of the sky?
And they don't come looking for me during night?

Why is that I see them longing for you
even in my presence? And find solace at my
departure.

CELESTIAL REFLECTIONS
a cosmic dialogue,
moon's reply

Why do you seek the attention of
the empty minded.
You exist without me and without you
I am just a rock being held by
the command of Allah.

If they write of me they write of you.

You light up the sky during the day
and secretly throughout the night,
do not attempt to study the minds
of the uneducated; you to will be
like them my dear.

Do you think the gazelle
appreciates the lions presence?

No.

Do you think the lion welcomes
the gazelles presence?

Absolutely.

You are my gazelle and you're their lion.
I chase you for light and you
chase them for attention.

The faster you run the more
I am in tune with my phases and
when you return to Allah I become whole.

Do they not see me in day time
admiring your eminence?

If you love me my brightest star
then let us be face to face leaving
the world into a total eclipse.
Only then would they admire us equally.

- sinnerspen

Parting Hopes
A promise in nature's embrace

If Allah wills we will cross paths again
On a path where autumn flowers fall,
with a gentle breeze of the first rain,
with a cool setting sun,
chirping of birds in the background,
and with a hanging moon behind the rainbow.

If Allah wills we will cross paths again.
Again in the most beautiful way where
everything in the nature bear witness.

As I bid Farwell to you..

HUES OF HEALING

Your bruise is a fine art,
with tints of pain,
with hues of blue, purple;
red, and black.
Memories cascade in
with every tender touch.
The color spectrum of a bruise
often leaves me in awe
of how exquisitely
my painful memories
are etched upon my body.
With each shift in hue,
my pain wavers,
now fading, now flaring
with each subtle change.
Yet this captivating art
destined to vanish
with passing time,
serves the reminder of
the beauty woven into
every experience and
the transient nature of existence.
Let your pain meld into
the shades of red and blue,
dissappearing along with the
fading bruise.

IN THE SHADOWS OF UTTERANCE
Navigating the Beauty and Bruises of Bullets and Words

The bullet, once unleashed, can never retract its course, rendering itself useless after piercing a soul, drenched in the profound hues of spilled blood.

Likewise, words spoken from the heart, once released, echo eternally, shattering the very core. The wounded soul remains amidst the debris of harsh expressions.

Choose your words with the tenderness of empathy; let them be a balm, not a wound. Speak kindness or let the serenity of silence embrace the moment.

AUTUMN AFTER RAINS
A Poetic Reflection on Seasons and Emotions

Autumn rains are gentle.
This autumn was a
mixture of seasons.
Autumn is warm and cool;
wet and dry.
Autumn is like
the way it feels after rain..
Serene, calming,
loud with birds chirping
Awaiting for new beginnings

Autumn after rain resembles
to you after you cry.

While raining, you could only hear
the droplets falling, the lightning, and thunders
Everything comes to at pause,

People stepping out, waits
People traveling, pauses
People returning, holds longer

Once it's over,
Everything resumes.
Feels strange and new when
you start hearing crowds of noices
With bits of sun and breezing air,
and with falling leaves

It's same when you cry
You only hear
your inner thoughts, as droplets
people's taunts as lightening
their behavior as thunders

Once it's all out,
The emptiness your eyes carry,
the calmess your heart feels,
the feathery your soul feels,
Just as the tree which
shed it's leaves
We shed our bad thoughts and
become an autumn tree,
With branches ready to bloom

Today, with the gentle rain again,
I waved my hands,
hoping for a rainbow again,
in the next autumn.

TALES OF MONSOON SERENITY
Dancing with Raindrops and Contemplating Dreams

Monsoon doesn't feel like one,
until it-finally rains
Tonight's rain was so calm as
it's each drop spelt serenity.
As soon as I heard the sound of rain,
I ran leaving my movie on pause...

The rain was gentle & warm
cool & serene, light & dark!
I wandered,
hiding in the darkness of night,
feeling safe and secure.
Cheering with the rhythm of rain,
hovering over my thoughts,
free from strains.

Seated by the door, on the sofa's perch,
Welcoming it, I let the cool breeze in
Unfurling my scarf in the cool air's dance.
Lost in the moment, in the nature's trance.

It came in as a gentle push,
which made me feel like
a dandelion, I felt stuck, not strong.
Wavering, and floating, in the air I sway,
Yearning to break free, to find my own way.
To blow away freely as others
but I guess what held back me was
my fears, uncertainties, and insecurities.
And amidst it all, the weight of expectations,
Adding to the burden, shaping my hesitations.

Stepping outside I saw a tree
in a playful motion
swinging in a funny way..
A quirky dance and a whimsical devotion.
I giggled at how weird & -funny it was.
But it made me realise that
people with dreams and goals
are like trees, whose roots are
strongly embeded with
sincerity, diligence;
consistency & discipline.
That no matter how strong
the storm hit them,
they still remain firm
and bloom gloriously

I truly admire them ☆

what are your memories with rain?

GRATITUDE

Be grateful for everything you possess and for every emotion you experience. Whether your prayers are answered or not, be thankful. Cherish the blessings you've received and the relationships you hold dear. And even in moments of emptiness, find gratitude, for it is in gratitude that we find true abundance and contentment. So, with a heart full of gratitude, embrace each moment, recognizing that every experience, challenge, and blessing is a precious gift from Allah.

SKY'S DELIGHT
Moments that Lift the Soul

Birds and butterflies are
enough to lift me up,
The sound of Plane
makes me jump around,
You'll find me searching
the whole sky just to
capture that moment,
The fireworks makes
my eyes wide open
in it's awe,
Moving along the sun,
makes my path brighter,
Peaceful mornings,
clouds drifting by,
pretty sunsets that paints the sky.

Moon highlighting you,
Sparkly hanging stars,
All bring me joy in the depth of the night.
Everything about you, oh sky, fills me with wonder.
To know what's hiding in your end.

Oh Sky, will you allow me to hug you and hold you near?

RAINY REVERIE
Conversations with My Rab

Sound of thunder makes
my heart skip a beat.
The stormy wind waves
through my hair, a fleet.
The first drop of rain
sparks excitement's flame,
I see roads emptying,
people seeking shelter
Where I seek mercy.
I stretch out my hands
facing skyward,
feeling the moment's demands.
Then I step out neath
the rains gentle pour,
close my eyes, raise my hands, and
my soul to implore.
Praising my Rab I make dua sincere,
Talking to Allah water rolls, a tear,
through my cheeks,
is it tears born of love for my Allah
or mercy bestowed in this moment's design?

Simply calling out to You, my Rab,
I find, When words fail,
Your presence fills my mind.
Then, as I open my eyes
to conclude my plea,
I raise my head, turn around, and see,

People bustling,
streets being busy again,
where I stand still, wishing
for a rainbow's score.

WINTER NIGHTS

Winter nights,
Under the rug snug,
Warm and cozy delight,
Clock's ticks loud, yet quiet the night.

Clear skies, darkness stark,
Peaceful, yet chaotic spark.
In the stillness, hearts unfold,
Contrasts blend, emotions untold.

Moonbeams dance on frosted ground,
Whispers of winter's silent sound.
Wrapped in blankets, snug and warm,
Embracing the night's tranquil charm.

Stars twinkle in the velvet sky,
As time passes in a gentle sigh.
The world outside, in peaceful repose,
While inside, the fire's ember glows.

In this haven, worries fade away,
As night turns to the light of day.
But memories linger, soft and clear,
Of winter nights, so dear and near.

DO YOU FEEL YOUR HEART TOO?

Our hearts feel everything, yet can we feel our hearts? I can. When happiness fills me, I sense my heart smiling, radiating joy. Acts of kindness bring peace, a gentle calmness that envelops my heart. Conversely, engaging in harmful actions weighs heavily; I feel a burden, as if a heavy stone or lock encases my heart, suffocating its light. And when I'm hurt, it's as if my heart plummets into an abyss with no bottom in sight.

In the ebb and flow of emotions, our hearts serve as faithful companions, guiding us through life's highs and lows. Despite the heaviness of pain and the weight of mistakes, there remains a flicker of hope, a reminder that our hearts possess the resilience to heal and flourish once more

CH 03
Tiny Tales

UNSPOKEN CONNECTIONS

A Silent Encounter at the Door

I heard someone banging at the door, I knew it was him behind the closed door, so I unlocked the door, and walked away. I saw no one coming in so I thought I may have mistook someone else to him. So, I ran through the windows, no one caught in my sight. I went back to the door, before closing it, I rechecked if someone was out there. And I saw him sitting on the stairs, with his head down. "What are you doing there?" I asked but couldn't pull it out my mouth. I stared at his back, wanting to ask him, sit next to him, pat on his back, and ask him to come inside. "He might stand up soon" I thought and walked away again, slowly. I stood behind the curtains to see him enter home, but he didn't.

A CUP OF TEA
Brewing Moments of Anticipation and Heart Flutter

'Make me a cup of tea,' he said. 'Okay,' I replied and rushed to the kitchen. Swiftly, I found the tea pan, placed it on the stove, added milk, sugar, and tea powder. As it boiled, nerves danced within me, wondering if it would taste good. Pouring it into the cup, I called his name. No response. Midway, I recalled his request for water! Turning back, I placed the tea cup and a glass of water on a tray. Standing there, I waited until he took his first sip, hesitant to ask how it tasted. Unable to resist, I finally inquired after he took a few more sips. 'How's the tea?' He nodded, and I retreated with a fluttering heart.

A YEARNING FOR CONNECTION
Unspoken Apologies and the Power of Kind Gestures

A kind gaze, a simple gesture, does alot!
It can erase all the bad qualities of that person.
I realised this long ago but recently it's been on my mind, that i wanted to relay this message.
I actually want to talk to her, a class fellow of mine. She's introverted or to be more exact chooses her ownself and her 2 friends over us. Well, that's fine.

To be honest at some point I wanna talk to her and apologise for all the assumptions I had [which might/might not be true] But I didn't.

It's been a year, we are still a class fellow, I would want to let her know but if not, I'll be letting it out here.

I don't just want to ignore her when we run through each other in the corridor, or find herself alone when I entered the classroom, I would atleast want us to close enough to greet salam. I do but maybe in a low voice that she doesn't hear, or maybe she answered in a low voice too.

She always felt distant, not to me, but to everyone. We would've made 1 year worth memories if only she loosened herself a little, or maybe we held our hands little longer for her to grab.

To be honest, I feel she's more awkward near me or I don't know. But recently on the nutrition day, when she brought noodles. Everyone were eating in one plate. She offered me chop sticks, I said 'No, I can't use them', she giggled and showed me how to use, then showed me another way to spin it and grabbed it in my hand, her little laugh when I was trying to eat with them, was so kind and warm which made me forget all the things/thoughts/assumptions I had for her.

I wanna talk to her and let her know, it's been on my mind since many days but I know I would not be able to do.

But there are some cases,
Where you will never forget the bad they've done to you
But a warm smile, a simple text, a smily gaze, would surely help you to hold on to them.
It'll help them to bear what's coming ahead.

STARRYY

a celestial love story in the night sky

Just like all the nights, you stare at the sky
Get amazed by the night sky filled with stars
You watch them, and be silly enough to count them
Although you don't know any of their names, or the constellations they make,
You love them, without their identify.
Just like a normal night of star gazing,
Wishing to see a shooting star,
Although you know deep inside that you ain't gonna see that, but one day suddenly a huge, shiny, star fell so fast with all it's rage
To be honest, I didn't realise that it's a shooting star, cause it was gone instantly
Then as my eyes were wandering throughout all the stars, I saw this star twinkling in a rhythm so similar to my heart, I stared at it's beauty, and "woww what a natural beauty" Is what my words uttered everytime I came across it. So I named this twinkling star "Starryyy" yeah, starryyy, the more you stress it the more it's filled with love,
Starrrrryyyyyyyyyyyyyyy
Hehe, Allahumma Barik
So? Curious of what happens next?

This starry made my nights sleepless as it kept me awake with its twinkling. I kept staring at it, talking to it the whole night, sometimes even falling asleep with my face turned towards it. We connected in many ways, twinkled together, and made many memories, but as you all know, how far a star is? Right? Maybe a million or billion years far? That's how we were. Even though our reflections were so bright on each other, we were very far apart.

That distance made us even closer, and we loved each other dearly. I see she is with her other stars, and I'm with my other friends. She has a different life, and mine is different. She has her chores of rotating, keeping her shine intact, hanging proudly in the sky, not letting the dark night scare her. I know her light will pave a way through all the darkness of the night.

Yes, there are other stars that shine brightly, even more than you, but you, my starry, will shine uniquely and be the most twinkling star for me, forever. I wish we never grow apart, even when life gets boring, even when there's nothing left to talk about. Promise me we will still stay here, and stare at each other. I truly love you, my starry, sweet as honey, annoying as a mosquito, old as my granny.

'she' in the next pages is me and every person who've been through similar situations.

SEEKING

She has her own dreams,
yet she prays to fulfill others'.
She loves the skies,
wondering how it feels to soar above,
even though she's afraid of looking down,
of the uncertainty below.

She's riddled with doubts,
with many holes in her heart.
Will she ever be able to fly?
She finds solace in walking beneath the
shedding flowers from the trees.
But she's unable to walk her own path,
for she hasn't found it yet.
She fears not discovering her purpose,
her true calling.
Will she be able to carve out her own path,
to create one where none exists?"

FRAGILE RESOLVE

She was always insecure,
perpetually waiting for others
before taking action,
only to be left behind.
Doubtful, she hesitated
in the face of decisions,
always deferring to others,
even as she harbored regrets.
She knows she lacks confidence,
unable to trust her own choices.

And so, she continues her journey,
grappling with insecurities and doubts,
yet ever hopeful that one day,
she will find the strength
to trust in herself and her choices.
For now, she takes each step forward,
knowing that the path to confidence
begins with a single decision.

LOST IN THE LABYRINTH

After all those researches and thoughts,
she finds herself unable to speak up her mind...
and she's back at the starting point.
Not knowing the end in her thoughts,
she feels tangled up, unable to find her way.
But she knows she still has a long race ahead,
its end unknown.
Yet, she must press on,
still needing to find her way,
still having to start the race.

Despite the uncertainty,
she understands that finding her path,
wandering, and feeling lost
are all integral parts of her journey.
Even after the long search for her goals,
she knows that discovering her path
is just the first step.
The real race begins when
she finally sets foot on the road ahead,
ready to embrace the challenges and
adventures that await.

Now let's skip to the stage when she finally took a decision.

Her journey begins here, after much contemplation; she's finally decided on her destination, where she'll be arriving, In Shaa Allah. Some are pushing her up, while others are dragging her down. She's overcome all the pushes and pulls in her life, in her heart, in her mind. She's aware that she'll be sacrificing her time, her age, her youth in sleepless and restless days. And that thought scares her. Sometimes, she's so fixated on her goal and believes she can make it to the end, but there will be times when she'll feel hopeless, lazy, and doubt her abilities. There'll come a time when she'll want to leave it all behind and drop out. But she hopes she won't be swayed by those thoughts. She hopes she'll stay firm, not discouraged, and rise again like a full moon shining brightly, fixing her eyes on the shinier Moon, shining brighter than anything else at that moment.

This, her making an intention, setting a goal, is just the beginning. It truly begins when she works hard towards it, prioritizes it more, and enjoys the process. Only then will it feel like a journey. It's going to be tougher than she assumed, it won't be easy, and she's not sure if she'll regret it. She's sick of overthinking, stressing over it, so she's decided to just start. Will she regret it? If yes, then is regretting later better than this stress and all?

She's acting confident now, but honestly, she's not. Being honest, she wants to live a life that is satisfactory, full of peace and enjoyment. She wants to explore herself, to know herself. She doesn't know much about herself... You would find her weird saying this but honestly she doesn't know much about herself. She even doubts herself, her intentions. She doesn't trust herself, she feels like she's a coward, she lies to herself, she doesn't know what kind of person she is. She doesn't even know the purpose of her life. There are many things she wants to know about herself. Will this journey be a way to find these answers? Will it be a good one? Or will she end up with another regret? Will she reach the destination? She wonders how she'll be looking through all these processes.

13-12-2021
12:42 pm

Even after the 4 months of writing the previous entry. She's still at the same place, crowded with thoughts, overthinking, etc. She just couldn't make her decision. She's too concerned and burdened about how her decision will reflect on her future life. She's too scared to choose. Well, it's the stress that no one could understand her. There are somethings which she never shared with anyone, the worries she has, the stress she was going through, no one knows. There were these stages where—

That's how she stopped there, keeping a known, forgotten mystery for her future self.

The next page describes her present life.

If it's not recorded or documented, it doesn't mean that it's forgotten. There were many voice entries where she could hardly speak; all it could record was her cry and silence. She fought many battles unknown to the people; the only witness other than her was her Lord. In this time lapse, she regretted a lot and reassured herself that what's happening is happening for the best. Many helped her, and she finally had to choose something which she hated a lot, a thing which she could've chosen long ago. But before this, she promised her Lord that no matter where He takes her, she will strive harder.

So, keeping that promise, she works hard, with the guilt and regret in her heart. But sometimes she feels grateful for how things turned out. After the past few days' experiences made her realize how weak her heart is, and this must be the reason why Allah changed and twisted her paths, or else she wouldn't be able to bear it.

She might have borne it or got used to it, but it just seems cruel and unfair to her heart. Although it's a thing which she truly admired and dreamed of, and it surely is amazing...

Now, at times she still feels pangs of regret and emptiness; she is content. She is grateful for every pain and for every second she went through in the past years.

Despite the weight of regret and the burden of choices, she has remained steadfast in her promise to strive harder, guided by the belief that every twist in her path serves a greater purpose.

Her words evoke a sense of gratitude for the pains endured, for they have sculpted the strength within her. Even amidst the lingering echoes of regret and emptiness, she finds solace in the knowledge that each moment, each trial, has shaped her into the resilient soul she is today.

In the tapestry of life, woven with threads of joy and sorrow, her story stands as a testament to the power of perseverance and the resilience of the human spirit. May those who find themselves in the depths of their own struggles take comfort in knowing that they are not alone, and that within every hardship lies the seed of growth and transformation.

Embrace your journey, for it is through the cracks of our brokenness that the light finds its way in.

CH 04
EVENING MUSINGS
unfurling emotions

AT SUNSET'S WHISPER
A Rush for Tranquility

As soon as the clock ticks '5'
my heart becomes restless,
runing around in search of my scarf,
become chaotic over which one to put on
As time's ticking I just grab my
regular white and pink scarf,
take the keys, ofcourse my mobile,
definitely my airpods,
Jumbling over the stairs...
and Hashhhh!!!!!!!!

Thankfully the sun is still up,
I keep my phone, keys aside and
Gently walk over the ground with bare foot..

I sat on the floor of terrace,
(which I normally don't),
cause I was out of breath.
Eyes on my Quran,
felt as if all the birds are chirping over
the words of Allah
 <as I was reciting out loud>

Then I furled myself like a cocoon,
didn't unfurl myself for the phone rings,
I heard.
I saw myself in midst of the birds,
as all I could see was sky!
Seeing those flocks roaming,
wished to get unfurl and fly like a bird.
Little did I know
that it was a fleeting moment,
that the sun would set,
which I wished to stay longer,
I stood up,
the sun turned red
like my blushing cheeks,
I quickly grabbed my things,
ran off to the stairs,
but paused for a final glance
on the setting sun.

MOMENTS IN THE SKY
A Reflection on Change

I ran upstairs to check on you
As I haven't for a while
I saw you covered but
could still see you shine,
I treasured this moment as
I sat down watching you
uniquely set down
by emitting shades of pink, green,
yellow and orange.
This view of yours made me fall
on the ground so I sat
leaning on the Pillar behind,
I let my feet feel the ground
so I wished to warm it
by patting, and stroking
through it's roughness
Made me feel it's softness
cause the sabr it had when
we stomped upon arrogantly
It chose to remain gentle
waiting for Allah's order
to burst out.

I soon opened my eyes
as soon as heard a plane,
My eyes followed it
till it was out of sight.
the moving clouds
caught my eyes,
They followed them,
until they realised that
they missed out how
the sky was welcoming
the new patterned clouds
(As it focused on what was leaving.)

Never be too focused on what's falling out of your hands,
Never be too focused on what's set to leave
As you'll miss out the chance
to welcome new beginnings on your way.

Do not walk with arrogance
Don't stomp but be gentle
Humble yourself as it's gonna be
Your final home.

EMBRACING SERENITY
A Glimpse into an Ordinary Evening's Beauty

It's strange how it feels
My notes app is open for a while now
And when I try writing
I just go back to the time
to re-live the moment
It's something indescribable
but I gotta force myself,
to preserve this memory.

I was so damn sleepy that
I decided to pass over
my evening walk but then
I got this feeling, that
I'll be missing on something
really beautiful today.

So, I ran upstairs,
the first glance at the sky
at those scattered clouds,
the hiding sun, and
I find myself capturing it.

As always, on my barefoot,
I walked around gently,
my eyes upon the sky,
And when I looked straight above,
I saw my most awaiting wish
infront of my eyes, A PLANE!
Finally..

This evening was ordinary,
yeah but with different
patterns of clouds
I sat down, leaning on the pillar,
The spot, from where you could only
see the sky, with no buildings n trees

It seems as if I'm an inhabitant of the sky
just floating in the air
watching the birds fly
making me wanna hug the sky,
to let my warmth speak
the love I hold for him.

While the clouds were revealing
the hidden sun, it's rays were
so gentle to my skin
just as a blooming flower
would feel.

With the birds chirping,
wind blowing, and the gentle sun..
It's as if I was witnessing
a sunrise during a sunset.
Which proofs that surely
there are new beginnings
at the end of each story.

I switched nasheed in the background
to the Quran, surah Rahman,
Everytime the verse is recited,

"Which, then, of your Lord's blessings do you both deny?"

I replied "NO, there isn't any blessing of my Lord which I deny"
with tears rolling down my cheeks

These tears didn't suffice my heart,
so I fell in the sujood, on the rough bare
ground, speaking hamd of Allah,
in His gratitude, Alhamdulillah.

Leaned back again, covered my eyes,
gathered my soul which was
dancing and giggling with the birds.
To return home, from a place
where my soul feels home.

The last SubhanAllah part of my evening
was when my eyes saw the sky turning into
the most beautiful shades of
pink, blue, and purple.
Endings are surely beautiful
Yet painful to depart

hamd : praise of Allah

SUN, RAIN, AND THE IN - BETWEEN
A Moment of Serenity

When I stepped out
I felt drizzling rain.
When I turned around,
saw it was raining,
with the sun up!

So I rushed upstairs,
my eyes searched the whole sky,
in hopes to see a rainbow,
but couldn't spot one.

I took off my slippers,
to walk barefootedly,
On the earth which
was just touched by
a gentle shower of rain.

I closed my eyes,
feelt the breeze,
which swayed my dupatta.
The cool breeze felt
so warm to my soul.

A huge smoky cloud,
made my feet adhered,
freed my thoughts;
leaving glimpse
of the shiny hidden sun,
seeing it reflecting on
the clouds close by.

A sky with yellow shades,
black and gray
white and blue (clouds),
fronted by the greenery
of the brown wooden trees.
And streets painted with
all shades of colours.

How can I complain now,
when life's filled with
rainbow colours, it's just us
who need to admire it.

But I still prayed
for a wishful rain again,
this time, with a
hanging rainbow.

Look!
I'm completely dazed,
and dazzled by
the vast sky.
I soon grabbed my phone
to capture it.
It almost fell off
from my hands as
my eyes followed
the moving clouds.

I stared at those moving
gray clouds brining forth
the sun and the glowy
white clouds.

I was dazzled by
the sun's rays,
gazing at it
became a struggle.
So, I stopped
stressing my eyes,
and allowed it to rest
by closing it gently.

I could feel it's warmth
hugging me and the
cool breeze brushing by me.
I stood for a while,
Being lost in the air.

I slowly opened my eyes,
saw the gray clouds
dispersed now and
the clear visible
warm sun.

I looked around,
it's shadow on
the houses,
the flowy
hanging clothes
drying again,
busy streets,
chirping birds,
vehicle's horns,
and children's laugh.
Made me realize that
I'm back again
to the reality.

So I put on my slippers,
went to my spot, sat there,
took out my phone,
opened my notes app,
to try writing
after a long time.

Soon after writing
one or two lines,
I saw water drops
on my screen,
I tilted my head
in an astonishing way.
Jumped down,
stretched my hands wide,
faced my head to the sky,
feeling the rain,
with the warmth of sun.
Which filled my heart
with hopes of
rainbow again.

I soon took off
my house shoe,
roved barefootedly
till the last drip of
the rainy cloud.

I came back, took my phone
which was hidden under the chair.
I sat on the ground, by leaning on
the pillar,
opened my notes app again,
and continued writing.

Which is now!
From down here,
I could only see
the dispersing clouds,
the setting sun,
the wandering birds, and
the swaying trees.

It's as if I'm draped over,
with the blessings of Allah.

I guess I should get up now,
put on my slippers,
to return home,
as it's time for the
sun to return, for the
wandering birds to return, and for
people to return.
Return to their homes

what makes you happy?

SEASONAL SHIFTS

New season, new winds, new beginnings..!

scorching heat turned to soft light, 5 Fan speed to 1-3 speed, cozy vibes under blankets, Heavy, sweet sleeps making me harder to wake up.

Still lost in the maze, and the answer of it is to find my spirituality, cleanse my heart, and make my imaan stronger.

27.06.2023

YEARNING FOR WINGS
a skyward reflection

The thing I envy most is birds—literally! Every time I look up at the sky, I wonder how it feels to examine it closely, to be so near those pretty clouds. I want to touch the clouds; these thoughts persist in my mind, even though I'm terrified of heights. Then, a bird enters the frame, capturing all my attention. I watch them fly, making circles, freely roaming and being closest to the sky. Ahh... I just want to fly aimlessly like them (I know they might be busy searching for food/shelter, but still). It's far better than feeling lost in this world. If only I had wings like them... Anyway, it's not possible, so I can at least rant about it, right? And thanks for listening!

FLIGHT OF SOUL
A Prayer Mat Reflection on Freedom and Hope

While observing birds gracefully soaring in the sky,
Seated on my prayer mat, leaning against the pillar, I sensed my soul taking flight alongside these winged creatures.
A weightlessness enveloped me, breaking the sense of confinement
My soul witnessed a multitude of birds, A flock crafting intricate patterns, Harmonizing in song as they journeyed homeward. Some swift, some in clusters, A few embodying both qualities, And others solitary, unhurried, not soaring too high, Yet disappearing from my view, perhaps destined for home, Don't you think?

SUNSET STROLLS
A Communion with Nature's Serenity and the Departing Sun

I call it my evening walk
But my feet are adhered
everytime they spot
the perfect spot
to spot the sunset

In those moments, a profound peace
envelops me,
comforting and consoling my soul,

My soul seems to intertwine with the sun's descent,
expressing gratitude for its luminous duty, acknowledging for a need to well-deserved rest.

The departure of the sun, a signal to the sky to paint itself in hues of breathtaking beauty, echoes a truth - that a setting sun is as pivotal as the rising one, marking not only farewells but also heralding new beginnings."

So, I won't name it as my evening walk,
It's more like a dose of nature's serenity
and a communion with departing sun.

JOURNEY OF COMPANIONSHIP
Navigating Life's Path with Memories and Smiles

Life is truly a journey,
We keep walking ahead,
No matter what
Be it a calamity or a blessing
Few pave their path,
While the rest simply move on
We encounter many people
There are few who become
our best companions,
The time spent with them,
is priceless, we assume
that they will accompany us
all the way our destination
However, as everyone has different routes
Departing becomes mandatory
Those we thought would
never be apart are now separated.
Those who couldn't imagine
living without each other are now distant.

Surely, they will remain the
best part of the journey,
And we presently enjoy the best
companionship,
And will find more on our further journey
All contributing to making
our journey bearable.

As said, we cannot walk down
the same path again
But we can pause our journey and
look behind, wave at them
with a gummy smile.
To let them know that they aren't forgotten

Who stays is you and your Lord alone.

Whether it's good or bad,
We can change our paths ahead
but can never walk down
the same road again

SUNSET UNSCRIPTED

Today was unexpected, feeling like a roller coaster ride. I didn't plan to spend my Friday evening at my favorite place, but my feet led me to it as my heart was always drawn there. Did you guess it right? My favorite place? Yeah! My terrace! Hah, I know you got it wrong, don't fool me.

Anyways, as I had time before my next exam, I thought to grab my newly acquired book, "Musings of Qalb," resting on my shelf for days. While the enchanting notes of my favorite nasheed played, I strolled with gentle steps, eyes on my book. I couldn't go beyond a page as my soul was magnetically drawn to the sun, clouds, and birds. Closing the book with my finger as a bookmark, I witnessed the beautiful sun shining beyond the concealing clouds.

Do you see that? We still tend to shine even when dark clouds cover us? As I moved forward, I saw the sun sliding down, captivating me. I planned to enjoy it while sitting on my favorite spot, but by the time I got there, just a couple of seconds later, the sun had completely hidden! Look, some things are meant to be enjoyed during our journey, as we might lose those moments forever when we reach our destination. So, look around and grasp all the moments you can, which later could bring laughter while seated on your throne of destination.

Then, a massive flock of birds covered the entire horizon, and I couldn't contain my joy as they flew above me. Although I missed capturing them initially, I enjoyed watching them until the end. While daydreaming during my stroll, my eyes caught a shiny object in the sky—was it a plane? A rocket? Attempting to capture it, my eyes followed, but it vanished into the clouds, eluding my sight. My heart pounded, pondering, Was it an angel?

Reflecting on how excited I get hearing and spotting planes, contrasted with the anxiety of them crashing, I imagined a plane crashing right in front of me. Did you brush off such thoughts, thinking they might jinx you? Now, consider the children who, instead of enjoying these moments, live in terror at the thought of losing hundreds in a single blow.

Every part of my day serves as a poignant reminder of Palestinians. Returning with a heavy heart, I prayed for them to experience the joys I take for granted.

GAZING BEYOND:
Evening's Unspoken Symphony

This evening was not painted with multiple colors, nor were there pretty clouds. But the sky had subtle tints of orange, blue, and white, enchanting in its serenity. The sun was so pleasantly beautiful, starting orangish and turning complete red. A rare moment when I could look the sun in the eyes.

My urge to hug the sky increased, feeling my soul enchanting in the air along with the notes of nasheed playing in the background. Watching the serene sunset, resting my chin on my hands. It was as if my soul stood at a window, peering out towards a realm where heaven resided.

In that serene moment, my thoughts wandered to Jannah, and I pondered how it might feel. The vision of a sunset in Jannah played in my imagination, and I was certain that my heart wouldn't be able to contain the sheer beauty of such a sight.

As the evening unfolded, the familiar backdrop of the sky was adorned with freely soaring birds, dancing and twirling in the air. Resembled Palestinian children
Their laughter echoed, and my tears fell with a bright smile. My heart couldn't contain the happiness and agony it felt.

Feelings of both joy and sadness swirled within me, a mix sparked by the sky's splendor, the laughter of children, and thoughts of the vast wonders in the heavens. That evening turned into a beautiful chapter inscribed on the pages of my soul, where the simple moments unfolded into something truly extraordinary.

IN THE SHADOWS OF YOUTH

Watching school kids pour out when the bell rang,
Stirring the calm street into chaos,
Filling the atmosphere with laughter and eagerness,
Experiencing a different sense of freedom.
Cycling home which meant more than a journey,
a few linking arms together forming a chain.
Families eagerly awaiting at the gate, waving,
indicating their parking spot,
A silent dance signaling the joyous reunion.

During my evening strolls,
I became an unnoticed spectator of their youthful escapades.
Where a sweet vendor is surrounded by little ones,
Forming little gangs, with a few left behind waiting.
My ears often catch their little funny tales,
innocent rants, and plans for the evening.

Yet admit this lively scene,
envy gently tugs at my heart,
Reminding me of a time when I, too,
was a carefree child.
I'm sure there must have been another Furled
Staring at me, envious of how lively I was.

Now standing at the crossroads, at a stage where the future me may envy, I find a pang of fear gripping my heart.
I realize that this cycle of life is unstoppable,
And change is undeniable,
Where envy takes different forms, leaving us no choice but to accept it.

In this unfolding story, the characters weren't just the children on the street but also the unspoken emotions, a universal truth woven into the narrative—the unstoppable passage of time and the ever-shifting shapes of envy that accompany it.

SUNSET REVERIE
A Dance with Departing Feathers

Perfect sun, a flawless circle
blending orange and red.
I form an imperfect circle
with my hand to frame its beauty.
Birds mistake a kite for their companion,
circling around it.
Suddenly, a breathtaking spectacle unfolds
as a multitude of birds soar from every direction.
Above, birds treated me as their dancing puppet,
moving to the rhythm of their graceful flight.
Sadly, they departed, leaving me
with puppet strings in hand.
Waving and calling out,
I yearned to meet again,
under the vast canvas of the sky.
I rose on my tiptoes,
I reached for the last glimpse of the sun,
a fleeting moment suspended in time.
Filled with a rush of joy,
I leaped and hurried to the other side,
eager to extend a heartfelt wave
to the departing sun,
a silent farewell etched
in the canvas of the evening sky.
It's departure painted the sky
in hues of enchanting orange and purple.

CH 05
INWARD *echoes*

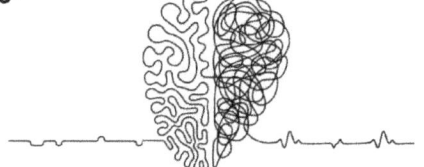

UNPACKING THE HEART

Today, amidst my tasks, a revelation unfurled,
Comparing life's burdens to setting up a world.

When you set up a room, or move into a different place, or just set up your dinner table, How do you do that? By making couple of trips? Get few more hands for help? By making rounds going in n out, up and down to set the whole thing., right!?

OBVIOUSLY YEAH!

BUT! Can you take them all out at once? CAN YOU? How possibly can one carry the whole set up with his 2 tiny little hands? No, right?

This time too! We will be needing all those rounds and trips but infact more! TO EMPTY IT OUT! ISN'T IT??

Then why do you expect the same with your heart? with your feelings? with your worries? with your problems? with your fears?

They just didn't come at you once! They piled up during the course of your life journey before you could even realise, now it looks like you're trapped, or it weighs you like a mountain!

So, do not try to flush them out in one shot, rather if you do that, you'll still can't be able to so!

Like for example, Even if you managed to grab all those things in your hands and you gotta go out, open the door of room/car, how could you?
You'll feel yourself loaded and trapped inside, right?

At that moment, you will still need to put some things down, right??? Or ask someone else to open the door for you, right?

Exactly! Don't trynna push yourself harder, just as time has piled up those worries/fears, with time they are all gonna flush away! In Shaa Allah.

So my dear yellow mellow, take things slowly, but infact enjoy it, pause in between to rest, and gaze the beautiful sunsets, if you're tired ask someone for help, to lend you a hand, the process might be slow but it will surely be alot more bearable than when you try it all at once.

And I'm damn sure that you're all gonna make it out, so soon, In Shaa Allah.

AND! I'M PROUD OF HOW FAR YOU'VE COME
/hugs/

GENTLE GLOW
Illuminating Character through Speech and Composure

A good person among the crowd is who, who shines through his manners, through the way he respects others, and the vibes he give off.

And the best among those are who, who controls his anger even when he has the right.

For me, I really pressure it alot, of how a person speaks, behaves, in front of others and in his house, when he's in best state and in his worst. As I know how few words can make your day, can also ruin your whole mood too!!

How many of us, acts "good kid" infront of strangers/outside. And "rude one" at his home? How many of us ask our siblings, parents, about how their life/day is going through? You never know what they might be thinking even when you live together. And how many of us, use harsh words addressing our younger ones? How many of you gets irritated when your sister/mom asks you to drop them, and you'll be ready if it's you going with your friends? How many of us lower our gaze/voice in the awe and respect for our parents? How many of us are patient when the other is yelling? (To not let the situation go out of the hand)..

Simply asking, "Khairiyth, how're you?" Means alot, effects alot! Giving a 1 rupee chocolate makes children smile. Teasing your sister will surely annoy her but will be her bestest memory, Offering atleast one salah at your home will make them feel connected. Or just simply sitting with your parents makes them feel happy. Sit with your brother not by just using your phones but by sharing eachother laughs.

Omar bin Abdul Aziz told his students,
"You should preach to others by your silence."
They asked, "How?!"
He replied, "By your manners."

Umar ibn Abdul Aziz

SINCERE STRUGGLE
Navigating the Battle of Intentions

Even though I start a thing with good intention, but when I recheck my Niyyah, I actually get confused! "am I doing it for Allah's sake or showing off?"

Recently I've come across a video, where it mentions, "A sign of sincerity is to always doubt your sincerity" and "A sign of insincerity is that you're sure about your sincerity"

This just blown my mind! You'll never win the battle against insincerity, it's an ongoing battle until we die. Anybody who thinks he's done with his battle, he's only lying to himself.

niyyah : intention

How to avoid Showing off:

1. Constantly checking your intention.

2. Gaining knowledge of "what's showing off?" about tauheed. The more knowledge we've the harder it is for shaytaan to deviate us.

3. Constantly asking Allah to cleanse your heart,

4. Increasing more private good deeds.

5. Reflecting upon your own shortcomings.

O' Allaah, make me better than what they think of me, and forgive me for what they do not know about me, and do not take me to account for what they say about me.

BELIEVER'S PARABLE
Believers as Kites in Allah's Skies

Just like kites,
Has an owner,
We believers,
Have Allah.
Just like how the owner observes it's kite,
How happy he feels when it flies freely,
Just like that,
Our Rab wants the best for us.
Even though the kite is his,
He won't let it go out of his sights
Cause he know someone might break their bond,
Just like that,
Our Rab wants His slaves
to be connected with Him
wherever he go!

The freedom a kite has, his own will to roam freely, to dance in the air, being in it's limits. And if due to any external things, it let go of his owners hand, it would have happiness, it would have freedom to go anywhere, cause there is no thread which connects it to it's owner,

Little did it know, that it's not gonna be longer, it'll eventually fall down, on an unknown place, feeling all alone.

Just like that, when a believer enjoys himself more in the pleasures of Dunya, being distracted by it's beauty or any other external things, he would slowly let go of Allah's Hand. And the beauty doesn't last more, he'll drift apart from his Rab, being lost!

But but! Do all kite owners simply let go of their kites!??? No, right!? They would search and find it, mend it, and let it fly again if he truly adores his kite!

Now, it's Allah! The One who loves us more that 70 mothers. Will He let go of us? Will he let us be in delusion? Will He leave His beloved slave all alone? Absolutely no!!

He would guide us, show us the right path, give us hidayah to seek forgiveness, and accepts our repentance. That's how Loving our Rab is! SubhanAllah.

RETURN TO MERCY
Embracing Forgiveness on the Journey of Imaan

Sin is inevitable
Imaan fluctuates,
we often walk away but
it is important to always return to Him,
regardless of how many times we leave
or how far we go,
so turn back because
you're always welcome,
Allah loves to forgive,
turn back no matter
how small the steps you take
seem to be,
turn back because
He will always be patient with you,
Even if you're impatient with yourself

"The heart of a true believer changes 40 times a day, but a heart of munafiqeen remains constant"

munafiqeen : hypocrites

THE ENGRAVED GRAIN
A Tale of Destiny and Trust in Qadr

My father repeats this saying every time, 'daane daane pe likha hai khane wale ka naam,' which means, 'The name of the eater is written on the grain.'

This time, he reiterated the same message when the guests were initially refusing to eat. My uncle then shared a story.

A professor had expressed the same idea, and one of his students asked, 'What if that grain has two owners?' The professor couldn't answer, as it was the first time he had pondered that question.

Later that day, they met at a party, shared a meal, and as they were about to wash their hands, the student who had asked the question coughed, and a few half-eaten grains came out. In the next moment, a bird swooped down and ate the remaining half of the grain.

The professor then said, 'Look, this is Qadr! That grain had two names written on it.'
The student was left amazed.
SubhanAllah, I loved this story a lot.

Through this story, I want to remind both you and me that whatever is in your Qadr will find its way to you, and you'll own it; no one else can.

If you've lost something—a relation, a bond, a precious material, anything—it was meant to be lost, and you were meant to part ways. I live by the motto, 'What happens, happens for the best.'

So, do not grieve over what has been lost, and do not yearn for what was never meant to be yours. Avoid exhausting yourself with regrets from the past and worries about the future. Reassure yourself that your Qadr is written by the best of planners; trust your Lord.

Lastly, remember that Dua can change Qadr, so do not give up on your duas. Make dua with firm belief in its acceptance.

Qadr : destiny; Dua : prayer

SACRED LONGING
Yearning for the Sacred, Unprepared for the Return

"I've always yearned for a place I've yet to set foot in. Tears of joy fill my eyes at the mere thought of casting my first glance upon the Kaaba. I find myself shedding tears as I wait, yearning for the moment my name is called. This dream occupies my thoughts during the day, at sunset, in my prayers, and even in my sleep.

Yet, amidst the eagerness and excitement, a realization dawns upon me—the journey is twofold.

How can I soothe my heart when departing from the blessed cities? How do I gather myself when every cell in my body has absorbed and dispersed into the sacred air of Makkah and Madinah? How do I resume my normal routine after my ears have been graced with the most beautiful adhan, my forehead has touched the holy land, and my hands and lips have embraced the House of Allah? How do I return to walking on ordinary ground after treading barefoot on the sacred lands?

Where do I find the peace that engulfed me in the city of our Nabi [saw]? How shattered will I be turning my back on those blessed places? How do I cope with the ache of longing when I'm thrust back into the realm of reality?

Yet, in this bittersweet waiting, I find solace —knowing that my heart has not yet borne the weight of departure, a weight still lighter than the restlessness I endure at this very moment.

[saw: sallalahu alaihi wa sallam; peace be upon him]

INTENTIONS FOR SPIRITUAL PREPAREDNESS

I've made two intentions that I thought I'd share with you all, with the sole intention of possibly helping you in some way, In Shaa Allah.

We-I always pray for umrah and Hajj, and am very eager to visit the blessed cities, so are we all.
So, I just got this thought, why not be prepared? We never know when we might be invited, cause most of them say 'they always thought of it, But it happened so quick and unexpectedly..'
Why not educate myself about it's rulings, duas, and the whole process?! And to know what to avoid, what duas to make and places to visit and make dua, like gaining knowledge on EVERY thing regarding umrah and Hajj along with their back stories. Also there are many such places which people tend to miss due to lack of knowledge or time, so if we plan and maintain notes we can avoid that, In Shaa Allah. Also regarding time management, having rough idea about the maps, and hotels..etc

This way our duas will have strong foundation, I mean we can pray with more firmness and tawakkul that Allah will surely call us.

The next one is –
As it's everyone's dream to memorise Quran, and May Allah let us achieve our goals. I got an idea, that till then, Firstly we need to memorize all the chapter names, and memorizing atleast three aayahs from each chapter so that we may recite it in our daily salahs! As it's three aayahs, we can look over it's tafseer and get a rough idea of the whole chapter.

This way, we can increase our connections with both Quran and Salah!
In Shaa Allah

May this be helpful to you

SOULFUL SUMMONS
Allah's Love in the Melody of Our Calls

This evening, the sweet sound of my niece repeatedly calling 'ammi, ammi...' filled the air. As we all know, moms don't always reply promptly, adding to the adorable persistence of her calls. Her innocent pleas were so charming and endearing; I couldn't help but think, 'Ah, my mom will surely feel so good and grant her every wish.' The mere melody of her calls melted my heart. In that moment, a beautiful realization dawned on me – this interaction mirrors our connection with Allah. Visualize how Allah must feel when His devoted servants earnestly call upon Him. It reminded me of a profound insight I once heard in a video – that Allah cherishes the cries and supplications of His slaves, hence, the delay in answering their duas. SubhanAllah. Reflecting on this, I recalled how I ask my niece to call my name, say 'please didi,' and give me a kiss before receiving her chocolate – a reflection of the love in our connection. Likewise, there are moments when we find ourselves whispering 'Allah, Allah...' and shedding tears on our prayer mats. SubhanAllah.
HE loves us abundantly /inserts heartfelt emotions/

didi: sister

CHRONICLES OF GRATITUDE
Finding Joy in Life's Everyday Chapters

"Days, months, and years continue their swift journey, while my life seems momentarily at pause. Yet, I'm grateful for every mistake, despite the regrets—they've been my invaluable teachers.

Alhamdulillah, Alhamdulillah! Words can't capture the depth of gratitude in my heart. SubhanAllah, my heart is never silent. As I grow in gratitude, my desire is to see those around me smile and laugh. Hence, I never miss a chance to share memes with my friends, even if it might make me seem a bit cringey. The joy it brings them is all that matters!"

I never had a particular fondness for cats, but seeing how much my friends love them, I started appreciating them, especially since they were the Prophet's (sallallahu alaihi wa sallam) favorite. Yes, I admit I get a bit nervous when they get too close.

Ah, children! They unfold countless lessons, Alhamdulillah. Trying to decipher what goes on in a child's mind is like handling delicate treasures - always 'handle with care/love.'

I've always been a 'sky person.' There's something enchanting about lying on the grass and gazing at the sky. Thankfully, I manage to do that on my way home, Alhamdulillah. I listen to birds chirping, relish breathtaking sunsets – moments others may not be fortunate enough to experience. Alhamdulillah.

I once had a goldfish, SubhanAllah. Although its time with me was short-lived due to the lack of an oxygen pump and the right water temperature, I had to change its water every two days and clean the marbles with salt. Yet, pondering on how Allah takes care of fish in vast oceans, even those in the depths receiving sustenance, is truly awe-inspiring.

From doing house chores and helping my mom to hugging her and enduring the occasional irritation when my sister nags, to sending them off and ensuring their safe return—every moment is a precious part of life. Waiting eagerly at the doorstep when I hear my dad's scooty, greeting him with a big smile, taking milk from his hands, asking about his day, massaging his legs, running my fingers through his hair until he sleeps, and kissing his forehead while assuring him that 'tomorrow's going to be all okay, daddy.'

Standing in the balcony, observing the street, hiding when spotting any boys, walking, thinking about all sorts of things, reciting nasheeds—just being ME!

A BIG ÀLHAMDULILLAH for the beautiful tapestry of life.

- Life unfolds when we open ourselves to appreciate the interests and passions of those around us. Just as I grew to appreciate cats through the eyes of my friends, embracing diversity in perspectives enriches our own understanding of the world.

- In the journey of life, we encounter fleeting moments, like my time with the goldfish. It's a reminder of Allah's care for even the smallest creatures. Just as I strived to care for the fish, let's reflect on the vastness of Allah's provision. Amidst challenges, be grateful for the lessons they bring. Remember, gratitude transforms ordinary moments into extraordinary blessings. Let's navigate life with a heart full of gratitude, finding beauty in every step.

So, let's treasure each moment and live with a resounding ALHAMDULILLAH for the blessings of the present. As we journey forward, let's carry the lessons of appreciation, gratitude, and joy in our hearts.

PAVEMENT POETRY
a contemplative pause in the symphony of urban life

While strolling along the roads,
Just after I crossed the pavement,
A heartfelt scene unfolded before me
An elderly couple navigating the path
with delicate steps
The gentleman who was challenged by mobility,
tenderly held his companion's hand,
gesturing to the traffic,
somehow managed to reach
the other side of the pavement,
Alhamdulillah.

In that moment, I found myself still,
halting my journey,
captivated by their gentleness.
Admist this several rickshaws approached,
mistaking me as a potential passenger.
Nevertheless, my attention remained fixed on the elderly duo
Perhaps a sense of concern or a desire to
witness their safety enveloped me.
They walked towards a fruit vendor
I trailed behind observing them on the other side
of the pavement.
I offered a silent prayer.
My gaze forward as caution prevailed
in the midst of bustling thoroughfares.

LOVE'S ALCHEMY
Eternal Transformations

In the quiet corners of my thoughts, the concern of love fading often lingers. Yet, I've uncovered a profound truth – Love is not a fleeting echo, it's a captivating transition.

It transforms into poetic gestures, delicate care, or merely the serene presence quietly standing beside you.Love, it appears, is an artful alchemy, painting itself onto the canvas of our existence, shifting shapes but never truly vanishing.

LOVE'S TAPESTRY
Expressions Unveiled

In the intricate tapestry of love, each person paints their unique expression...

Some convey it with warm hugs and kisses, devoid of any awkwardness.
Others show their love through actions, emphasizing the weight of your words and paving ways to support.
A few show their concern by scolding you for unhealthy eating habits.
There are those who consistently correct you, steering you towards growth.
Some willingly sacrifice for you
Becoming fuel to your success.
Others seems cold but lash out when someone hurt you, going beyond to protect.
Selflessness define some souls always putting you first.
Certain individuals who crafts delicious food with love.
Some carve precious time out from hectic schedule
Dua is the language of love for a few.
Letters sent your way with love..

Few are reminders of your worth, serve as timeless expressions.
Some makes you feel truly beautiful.
Few stand by you in moments that demand strength.
Some holds your hand through waves of anxiety.
Some catch your mood the moment you meet.
Others engage playfully, occasionally teasing and friendly fights.
Endless annoyance, strangely heartwarming, defines some relationships.

In the quiet embrace of someone's presence, love resonates. And these are merely a few notes in the symphony of love, a composition that could go on infinitely, with countless expressions yet to be discovered.

Hence,
the reason why we must be attentive to the details, cause those silent lovers are usually speaking volumes in those mostly unnoticed details.

In my heart's quiet moments, I ponder what my love might be...

Is it like the soft hug of a warm breeze, gently touching the soul?
Or maybe it's as cozy as a favorite blanket, wrapping comfort around me.
Could it be like the sun's warmth, casting a golden glow on my feelings?
Perhaps it's a familiar song, playing sweetly in the background of my thoughts.

In these simple musings, I find that love is like a sweet, gentle melody, simple yet incredibly pretty, quietly humming in the corners of my heart.

WHISPERS OF MERCY

A Prayer for the Needy

How can a heart not tremble with mercy and gratitude, and not shed tears on our helplessness when witnessing the plight of the poor, the homeless, the broken, the sick, the blind, the struggling one, the lost one, the oppressed one, the revert...

The makham [place] the poor has, is the biggest! That if you get to know you would wish you were poor instead.

No doubt they get the hardest struggles
And their hearts are rich with patience
Surely Allah is Al Qayyum, The Sustainer.

Always have mercy upon them, always feed them, give them water, do not be harsh on them, if you can, school them, teach their children.

May Allah clothe them, shelter them, feed them, help them, protect them, cure them, heal them, free them, guide them, forgive them, elevate them and open doors of Barakah for them and for us, Aameen Ya Rabbul A'alameen.

And Alhamdulillah in whichever state Allah has put us.

May Allah bless us with what we do not have, and increase in our blessings,

May Allah protect us from poverty, and grant us strength and sabr in every trial,
aameen

May Allah help all the brothers and fathers to help provide their families,

May Allah help all the single mothers and sisters who provide their families,

May Allah bless us with enough so that we could help the ones who come to us,

May Allah protect us from greed and from being stingy, selfish, and arrogant towards them.

May Allah open our hearts, and soften it with love and care; Rehma and sabr.

Aameen Ya Rabbul A'alameen

Let's unite in prostration to Allah and express our gratitude for everything, for the ability to empathize with the pain of others, and for the gift of gratitude, In Shaa Allah.

In these times, where sincerity can be compromised by deceit, let's earnestly pray to Allah for protection from those who may harm others by pretending to be in need. May Allah shield us from such individuals. Aameen.

REFLECTIONS IN INK

As I revisited my diary today, I stumbled upon entries penned during challenging times. I vividly recall the struggle, and interestingly, the only way I felt heard was through those written words.

There were few entries filled with sorrow, pain, and displaying how lonely I felt. And few entries which were filled with joy, excitement and fun. I cannot recall those moments, left me wondering about my own past self.

Guess that's life! No matter the intensity of the struggle, the heights of happiness, or the anxiety about the future, we tend to forget. So, don't fret about anything; focus on the present, for those moments won't return.

Surprisingly, even after years, I find myself standing on the same point. The words written then perfectly summarize my current emotions. It's similar to a father returning home empty-handed while his son awaits a present – I'm that empty-handed father to my past self. Yet, what truly matters is the safe return. Alhamdulillah for my present self. Just like fathers venture out for their families, I earnestly wish and pray that this ongoing journey brings waves of joy, illuminating our homes.

SOULFUL REFLECTIONS

Longing to meet my Maker, my soul yearns deep,
To converse, to inquire, in His presence to steep.
Yet, amid blessings, I tremble with fear,
Am I truly grateful, is my gratitude sincere?

For every gift bestowed, Alhamdulillah I say,
But fear grips me tight, will they be taken away?
What if Allah tests what I hold close and dear,
Am I prepared to face it, with faith clear?

But then I recall a comforting decree,
"Gratitude increases blessings," I see.
So, I lift my hands in hopeful prayer,
Trusting Allah's mercy, His love to share.

With each passing moment, I'll deepen my praise,
In anticipation of His compassionate gaze.
For in gratitude lies a divine key,
To unlock blessings, abundantly free.

FINDING WHAT YOU'VE FOUND.

Being born into any religion is not the end of the journey; instead, one needs to find their true religion. Cultural practices often obscure the authenticity of one's faith, requiring individuals to unfurl these layers to let the true essence of their religion shine through. From my personal experience, it's challenging to accept and refrain from practicing certain cultural norms, and at times, it's frightening to seek the truth. It feels like I'm being tossed around like a ball, influenced by others' beliefs. This overwhelming feeling sometimes leads me to pray to Allah for guidance, whether it comes through a friend, a teacher, a guide, or my spouse. The fear of not finding anyone to guide me is real. However, I've noticed that any doubts or misconceptions I've had are often cleared with Allah's help. Many times, I come across posts claiming that certain beliefs are not supported by hadith, which initially may be hard to accept. And I just simply brush it off. Yet, after a few days, Allah provides evidence, reminders, or guidance through various sources that help me accept the truth. It's truly amazing and fills me with gratitude (SubhanAllah).

There are SO many things to educate ourselves about, to spread awareness. The main difficult part is to act upon it, to face your family and explain them. It's tough. May Allah make it easy for us to spread awareness. And May Allah bless them endlessly who helped me in my journey.

what are you grateful for today?

To be honest, the space here isn't enough to list all the blessings we have. Why not start with ourselves? Our entire body – our metabolism, our organs, their functions, our movements, our responses to stimuli, our power of thinking and decision-making, our conscience, our feelings, our senses, and much more!

Take a moment out of your schedule, seclude yourself for a while, and reflect on and appreciate all the blessings you have.

GRATITUDE CHRONICLES
Living the Duas

I've always questioned my present,
Every minute, every second, a relentless quest.
Yet, it often leaves me internally distressed.

Lately, I stumbled upon a saying,
"You're living one of your duas," it kept replaying.
But I shrugged it off, never truly conveying.

Yet tonight, a surprising wave engulfed me,
And I realized, indeed, it's meant to be.
I revisited my diaries, reflecting on what I see.

Yes, I'm much the same as I was before,
But circumstances shifted, and so much more.
Late as it may be, I see what I implored.

If only I'd been more positive back then,
Praying for better outcomes, and when
I contemplate, perhaps I'd have gained then.

But what if I alter my perspective's view?
What if I pondered, "Where would I be if not here, too?"
Surely, it'd be worse, a thought to construe.

So, Alhamdulillah a'la kulli haal!
For every circumstance, big or small.

So, why not take a moment, and introspect?
Revisit memories, with no aspect to neglect.
Change your viewpoint, what you reflect,
Even the slightest change, it's worth the effect.

CH 06
FOR US
an extract from my diary

"Peace be upon you for what you patiently endured. And excellent is the final home."

Hey mini diary,

I'm back again ^^ Alhamdulillah, it was a good day—my favorite day of the week. I experienced my most awaited moment and had fun with crackers, Alhamdulillah. Today, I want to share something with you: there will be times when you love, admire, or even hate yourself, and sometimes you may feel frustrated with yourself. During those moments, it's important not to blame yourself or your circumstances. Remember, Allah wants you to experience every emotion, every challenge, for there is a hidden message in each trial. Hold on to your faith, and let your light shine by helping, loving, and smiling at those around you. Your actions will reflect back to you, so don't forget to love yourself and prioritize your own well-being—you deserve it.

05.11.2021

Adhakallahu sinnaka
May Allah keep you smiling ^^

My mini diary,

Today, I learned something valuable: that fear of failure, of not being good enough, often dissipates once you muster the courage to try. What once seemed daunting, like a towering mountain in front of you, becomes more manageable as you take the first steps. With each attempt, you gain experience, confidence, and a sense of accomplishment. However, I must admit, I haven't quite mustered the courage to apply this principle to learning Physics and Chemistry just yet.

9.11.2021

Allah is with you,
Your ease is written,
Your happiness is written,
Relief will arrive,
And you will forget your grief.
Until it arrives,
O beautiful heart,
Observe patience,
Allah loves the patient ones.

Things don't always go the way you want. Every day, we navigate through a myriad of mental states – from stress and blankness to trauma, peace, or happiness. We may not always be aware of what others are going through, but we can reach out to them, stand by their side, and reassure them that everything will eventually be alright. A simple act of talking to them with a genuine smile, speaking kindly, can make a world of difference in their lives.

11.11.2021

Just like a painting,
It can't be complete with one stroke,
You need a few more tries,
Patience, picking your brush again,
Giving another stroke to make it beautiful.
Life needs a few more strokes too!
It can't be perfect with one,
You need to pick yourself up whenever you fall,
And start over for your life to become complete and beautiful.

12.11.2021

Allah is testing you by delaying your works, not stopping them. He's testing our patience and reliance on Him. I'm here to remind you that I know you've endured a lot and been patient through it all. Don't give up now when the end of this suffering may be near. Keep your faith strong and trust in Allah's plan.

Dear me,

Even in the midst of being stuck, remember to smile from time to time. I know you've always been grateful for having limbs to move, eyes to behold the beauty around you, ears to listen to the recitation of the Quran, and a tongue to utter the words of Allah. Take care of these blessings, for they will testify for you.

Perhaps the reason things are taking longer than expected is because Allah wants to grant you even more happiness. So have faith that you will emerge from this situation, In Shaa Allah. Trust that whatever awaits you is the best, so there's no need to worry about the future when it's in the hands of the One who created you!

Keep smiling, dear self. ^^

15.11.2021

There is no need for you to grieve over it except your religion if it is lacking, your faith if it is broken, and your shortcomings with God.

Dear me,

It's been a while, hasn't it? Well, things haven't been great lately, but there have been moments of happiness amidst the struggles. Alhamdulillah, I'm healthy, and that's something to be grateful for. I know you're going through a tough time right now, but remember, there's a greater reward waiting for you, In Shaa Allah. So hold on a little longer.

To all those battling their own struggles, remember, you'll soar higher just like these balloons! In Shaa Allah. So don't let go of the hope you're clinging to right now. ^^

Thank you, and goodbye.

02.12.2021

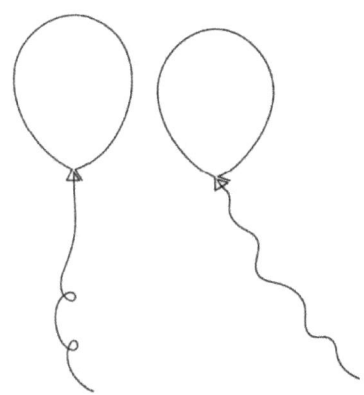

Found this in my gallery, and I just loved it!

They asked her,
"What does letting go mean"

She answered,

"Letting go does not mean erasing a memory or ignoring the past. It is when you are no longer reacting to the things that used to make you feel tense and releasing the enrgy attached to certain thougts. It makes self awareness, intentional action, practice and time. Letting go is the act of getting to know yourself so deeply that all the delusions fall away. "

credits to the owner

Hey my dear self,

I know the stages you've been through, the challenges you've faced alone, keeping them to yourself. Now you've reached a stage where you're sad, where you want to weep and feel frustrated, yet strangely, you're at peace. I don't know what this means, but despite the chaos and the thoughts swirling within, you're finding a sense of calm. You can't cry when you want to, and it's weighing on you. Whatever it is, I hope it ends soon, and most importantly, I hope you don't lose your Imaan. You may feel like you're drifting away, but I pray you find your way back to your purer self. Remember, you're not alone in this journey. There are others out there experiencing similar struggles, finding solace in the fact that they're not alone can be a comforting thought. In Shaa Allah.

16.12.2021

I know you might be feeling hopeless, experiencing guilt and regret somewhere deep in your heart, but do not let it consume you. Don't allow it to steal your precious moments with your loved ones.

Hey [Name],

I know you've been struggling with your Imaan lately. You've made countless promises to your Rab, vowing not to repeat the same sin again, committing to pray all prayers with sunnah and nafil. But then, the very next day (or after a few days), you find yourself breaking those promises. You live with guilt, your heart unwilling to repeat it, but it's become a habit... ingrained in your hands/ears/eyes. It's going to take time. I know you feel like you can't face Allah with the things you've done. But no matter what you've done, how many times you repeat, or how many promises you break, remember you still have a chance until your last breath. You can promise to your Rab again! You can start again. Please do not lose hope, for that's what Shaytaan wants from you.

Ya Rab, we again promise You that we will try our best not to repeat it. Even if we do, please do not stop giving us guidance. And Ya Rab, pardon us, our family, our friends, our Ummah.

It's okay, have faith.

17.12.2021

Assumptions and Expectations;
if you leave them you'll be at peace

Hello again!

As I mentioned before, breaking certain habits can be challenging, but I have a few tips that, InshaAllah, can help you stay away from them.

1. Fasting:
Have you noticed how pure you feel during Ramadan? That's because of fasting! Fasting not only keeps you away from sins but also constantly reminds you of Allah. It's a time when you restrain yourself and engage in more good deeds than usual.

2. Set yourself a punishment:
Tell yourself that if you repeat the sin once, you'll offer 2 rakats of Salat ul Tauba. If you do it twice, then 4 rakats of Salat Al Tauba.

3. Replace it with a good habit:
Dhikr! It's the best. Yes, it's not easy to get into the habit, but here's a tip! Carry a tasbeeh with you at all times! Wear it on your wrist or keep it in your pocket so you're reminded to use it. Trust me, it really helps! You'll find solace in your own company, talk to Allah more often, and feel grateful when you see Allah's creations in daily life.

18.12.2021

EMBRACE YOUR STRENGTH

In the quiet storms you've weathered,
In the shadows where you've fought,
Amidst the tears that fell unbidden,
You've shown the strength that can't be bought.

So be proud of your silent battles,
Of the moments you've humbly braved,
For in wiping your own tears away,
You've shown the strength that can't be swayed.

be content with
what you've right
now.

"What if it doesn't work..?"

Navigating these thoughts is tough—it's a stage where self-trust wanes and capabilities feel uncertain. Almost everyone passes through this phase at least once in their life, and if not, they will! If you're in this stage, don't dwell too long, as it only makes reaching a conclusion harder. But I know you'll overthink it (cause I did ^^"). When your mind is occupied, share it with someone who can listen every time you need to talk. You'll gain clarity. Remember, you've Allah who can listen you even before uttering.

04.01.2022

Another reason why cleansing your thoughts is necessary is because the way you think affects your subconscious body's reactions. If you fill your mind with negativity, you'll receive negative outputs, and vice versa.

Additionally, a believer should always purify his thoughts and intentions for it may lead you to either good or bad deeds. Your mind serves as the root of both evil and good.

So, just brush it off whenever you think of something bad, get up and busy yourself with something good.

Moreover there are certain virtuous acts that may seem challenging to achieve, but simply make an intention and Allah will make it easy. [plus you already get rewards for only making an intention, hehe]

Change the perspectives of your 'ifs'

"What if it all works out?"

"What if today goes unexpectedly well?"

"What if the best is yet to come?"

"What if great things are on the way?"

"What if you have what it takes?"

I stumbled upon these questions
which made me feel good

philosopher Epictetus :

"If you wish to be a writer, write. If you wish to be a philosopher, think; but cross out every thought that is unimportant. For thoughts lead easily to words, words to actions, and actions to habits – so, remember this and let nothing distract you. If you don't, then in the end you will have no real achievements to show, or talk about."

IN THE SHADE OF SELF-DISCOVERY

Lessons from Trees

I have a couple of trees near my house that always catch my eye. One is umbrella-shaped, and I find myself gazing at it after every fardh prayer—it's become a habit, almost instinctual. The other tree reminds me of Ramadan.

Now, these trees have seen better days; they're dried up and not as beautiful as they once were. But despite their current state, I still feel a fondness for them. I believe it's important to cherish and care for them regardless.

When trees shed their leaves, it's as if a veil has been lifted, revealing their bare branches and sometimes hidden nests or spider webs. Similarly, when we face moments of weakened imaan or struggle with depressing thoughts, it's an opportunity to see ourselves more clearly—to recognize our strengths and weaknesses.

01.03.2022

Instead of harboring self-hatred, we should strive to understand and uplift ourselves, seeking guidance from Allah along the way. Just as some of us collect falling leaves and store them in books, why not accept and cherish ourselves, flaws and all?

Even during challenging times, a little extra care can nurture growth. So, let's nourish ourselves with an added dose of love, care, and remembrance of Allah—because it's in His remembrance that our hearts find true peace. ♡

things will get better, trust me.

INVISIBLE TRIUMPHS
A Symphony of Hope for Your Unseen Efforts

your efforts are seen, your pleads are heard, your silence is noticed, your tears are counted, your relief is near, your sufferings has an end, your wait will over, you will hear good news, you will receive glad tidings, you will laugh till your stomach aches

have you ever observed how a hen walks?
I did, and I cannot unsee it.

WHISPERS OF HEALING

I've come to realize a hard truth: no person can mend a broken heart except Allah. No one else. My words may not hold much weight for you, but my duas will, always. Hugs

You know, someone once told me at the beginning of this journey not to care too much because they wouldn't be able to reciprocate the same for me in return. At the time, I didn't fully understand it. I brushed it off, thinking they were just avoiding me. But now, as I feel myself draining—literally draining, like in that GluconD ad where the sun sucks their energy with a straw—I get it.

It wasn't until I was completely drained that I realized the weight of those words. There were other things too that made my heart sink. In those moments, I wanted nothing more than to disappear from everyone's life and memories. I was so close to deleting everything. I wasn't in a state of depression, but it was a different feeling, one I couldn't quite express.

Over the weeks, I've had my ups and downs. But now, I feel charged—like I've been replenished by GluconD. And though I still feel my heart fluttering, I think it's enjoying the ride rather than being weighed down by the fall.

So, my friend, take heed. Who knows? Perhaps Allah has saved a parachute for us, or maybe He's giving us wings. Or perhaps, when we fall, we'll fall into the safest hands—His guidance and mercy.

To those also feeling drained, know that you are not alone in your struggle. It's natural to feel overwhelmed, and it's okay to step back when needed. Just as I've found solace in my journey, so too will you. Within you lies a reservoir of strength waiting to be tapped. Trust in Allah's guidance, for He alone holds the master plan.

Remember, just as I found solace in the journey of healing, so too will you. You are stronger than you realize, and with time, you'll find yourself soaring once again. Take comfort in knowing that Allah is with you, guiding you through every twist and turn. So, let go of worry and trust in His divine plan. You've got this! ^^

AND DO NOT LET THE PAST SADDEN YOU FOR IT CANNOT BE UNDONE. LEAVE THE GRIEF SO YOU COULD HOLD THE SMILES WAITING FOR YOU.
/hearts and hugs/
23.05.2023

BE THE LIGHT

Be an ear to someone who needs to share what they feel,
a shoulder for someone who needs to lean on,
an eye for someone who lost their way.
Be a shadow for someone who needs to feel secure,
a hand for someone who needs to wipe their tears.
Your presence can make someone feel better.

PERSPECTIVE SHIFT

Finding Gratitude in Everyday Chores

As I say 'perspective' turns the whole damn scenario up-down like..when I read this which says

"what a privilege it is to clean a home that was made dirty by a healthy child playing, to clean dishes because we got to eat 3 meals today, and laundry that needed to be done because we all have clothes to wear."

05.09.2023

THOUGHTFUL PURITY

Purify your thoughts, keep them good for a better outcome.

My mom stresses this alot, she always reminds us to think positive, to think good of yourselves, cause it affects your brain.

And almost all sins originate from a mere thought.

And you wouldn't change until you change yourself! That's up to you.!

EMBRACING THE GARDEN OF LIFE

Overcoming Regrets with Resilience and Grace

My biggest fear is having regrets.
It eats you up internally.

Regret is a weed,
It's root is deep,
is hard to reap,
leaves you weeping.

Regret is a weed
No matter how many times
you try removing it from it's roots
the many times it grows back

But weeds can be covered
with cover crops
Why don't you cover it up
with something more
worthy and deserving.

weeds are grown on barren lands
fill your barren hearts, and bury them
under the monuments of your heart.

I understand, it's really hard to leave regrets and move on. I've been through it. But my dear, will you be able to change it? No, right?

So please do not let it consume your present and leave more regrets for your future self.

Get over with it. You can, my love!
Accept it, appreciate it for the lessons you've learned from it, and wave it with a smile and Bid farewell.

A reminder :
　　　Save yourself from harboring more regrets in the future—GET UP or PICK the phone and mend your relationships, uphold the ties of kinship— your friend, neighbor, parents, sibling, or relatives. Forgive. Seek forgiveness if it's your fault.

　　　Cherish and respect them as if they were no longer here, so that your love may endure without causing harm.

PRESENT TENSIONS
The Struggle of Living in the 'Now'

Isn't it ironic how we often don't appreciate the present moment, yet we long to relive the past or daydream about the future? It's as if the present bears the brunt of our dissatisfaction even though it's simply the transitional phase between the future taking over the past.

-ryt.rng

Allah's plans are best ♡

THE SILENT SYMPHONY
Cultivating Kindness in Words and Tears

"If you can't be kind, choose silence, PLEASE! The impact of 'the look' you give and 'the words' you choose can be deeply hurtful, often unnoticed. Regardless of your mood or the challenges of your day, strive to treat others, especially your loved ones, with compassion. And when you're hurting, don't bottle it up; let the tears flow, finding solace on your prayer mat. Keep some tissues nearby. Goodbye."

26.08.2023

HEARTFELT CARE

Nourishing Your Soul with Love and Dhikr

Take a break.
Take your time.
Talk to yourself.
Take care of your heart.
Feed your heart with best things so that it can grow stronger.
Remove alll unwanted things.
Always, every second keep your heart busy with dhikr.
And tune your music with quran.
Replace everything with something good.
That's how you take care of your heart.

Dhikr: Remembrance of Lord

BEYOND THE SHADOWS
Finding Comfort in the Promise of Ease

Brighter the light, darker the shadow.
Just as the brighter the days ahead
the harder the struggle gets.
Just when life gets too hard
and you're standing at the brink to quit,
know that the ease is near,
For Allah promises :
Indeed, with hardship [will be] ease.
Ash-Sharh 94:6

4.06.2023

Understanding someone's pain doesn't obligate you to solve it or be held accountable.

THE UNCERTAINTY

Finding Comfort in the Journey of Not Having It All Figured Out

It's okay to not have everything figured out.
It's okay to be lost.
It's okay not to be loved by everyone.
It's okay not knowing where to head.
It's okay to be aimless.
It's okay to not have any hobbies.
It's okay to wander.
It's okay to be home.
It's okay to be blank.
It's okay to be confused.

IT'S OKAY!

You'll eventually pull yourself through this, trust the process, trust your instincts, and go with the flow.

SPARKLY HOPE

It's truly a blessing when you talk about your dreams/goals [obviously to your loved ones] even when things aren't in your favour, but the hope you've!!! Is TRULY A BLESSING..
Like it's ALOT better than giving up and loosing hope

Sometimes it seems like life's being sprinkled by yellow gliters

Which doesn't really mean that it's all happy-happy, it's being hopeful in whatever the situation is.

So, it's okay even if things aren't working out for you right now, it'll somehow, someday, sooner or later, In Shaa Allah ☆°
Do not let go of that tiny sparkly hope you've in your heart ♡

2 PHASES OF EXISTENCE
Dancing as a Feather in Delight and Floating as a Rock in Sadness

I've two major phases
One, a super, delight, happy, and light one.
Where I feel like a feather, so beautiful, so elegant
[fine you didn't need to finish the line]
Yeah! So I feel like a feather, floating, dancing, flying in the air, smiling for no reason, tapping my feet, blushing, and being delulu..
[another trend, delusion*]

And the other phase, a really sad one, which can begin anytime anywhere for no reason! I feel like a rock, falling deep in the ocean. Everything weighs me down, but remember, when a rock weighs much it floats up! So will you and I!

26.11.2023

LIFE GOES ON..

"Life goes on. You'll move on. The worry of living without someone is futile, perhaps. By the moment you declare, 'you can't go on without so-and-so,' you are, in fact, going on! Because the matters that weigh heavily, the ones you stress or fret over, often unveil themselves as 'not so significant after all.'"

When your mind is crowded, unclear, or confused, try ironing your most wrinkled clothes

NOT EVERYONE'S BURDEN IS YOURS TO CARRY

Sometimes, you may not be able to lessen their burdens, especially if they are emotionally burdened.

It eventually affects you in a way you might not notice. Overcaring and overloving will just drain you out. Be there for them, pat them, and remind them that everything's going to be alright. Pray, and you're done with your part.

Don't let their burdens make you feel incapable of helping them. In fact, you're doing well. Do what you can and leave them in Allah's care.

Above all, take care of yourselves.

April 10, 2024 - Last day of Ramadan.

I had planned to seclude myself this Ramadan and give it my all, but unfortunately, I couldn't stick to my plan. Halfway through Ramadan, I felt overwhelmed, drained, and fed up. I couldn't understand what was wrong with me until I suddenly felt the urge to remove all distractions—and I did just that. No social media, not even WhatsApp. No entertainment, not even YouTube. I even took a break from college for a month. It was just me, my Creator, and my home.

Let me tell you, the peace and serenity I found in this solitude are indescribable. It feels like I could live this way forever. My mind and heart are clearer than ever, and I can tackle multiple tasks with ease. I've learned to use my time more effectively, although I've made sure to avoid oversleeping.

I would wholeheartedly recommend this experience to anyone feeling drained. Sometimes, all it takes is some time alone with your thoughts to find the clarity and peace you've been searching for.

I asked around this question - "what would be your message if it were to reach everyone in the world?" And listed down few of their responses-

"I'd want everyone to know that resilience often emerges from adversity, and seeking support is a sign of strength, not weakness. You're not alone, and there's always potential for positive change."

"Endure the pain, for Allah never wastes the reward of those who do good the hereafter is better than this life and your sufferings will soon come to an end Ameen"

"Have patience (sabr).. Eventually every sufferings ends with a reward. No matter what, don't loose hope. Almighty Allah is always there for you and He sees everything and everyone. (He is omnipresent)"

"Eat well" - my mom

"Don't feel alone because of your loneliness on the path of truth."

Quran 17 : 23-25

'go on, never stop. leave no place for regret'
'keep your tongue moist with isthigfaar and dhikr so you may live in goodness'.

'everything will be okay, it might not seem like it right now but, we and the world around us, change constantly. i promise you, it will pass'

"Know that Allah is watching and He is rewarding you for every second of grief you go though "

"Face it and fight it! Tell ur frnd to either fight for her right or make herself so strong that"

"There is no solution other than patience. For this is a test from Allah to His most beloved slaves"

"If something makes u happy it's not cringe or stupid, people who make u think like that are stupid "

"Mental health is real, depression isn't a weakness. Emotions are to be expressed."

"I would just say that don't lose faith and no matter what just believe in Allah"

One of them asked me back the same question

Well, having sabr, faith, trust and hope in Allah swt is obvious!
Apart from it, it's having mercy and being kind
Being kind with speech, through actions,
Being kind to yourself, your heart, your thoughts
Being kind to poor, to sick, disabled, orphans,
Being kind to parents, elders, teachers,
Being kind to children, and to strangers.

For me, character and respect comes first.

Also, knowing that YOU CAN ALWAYS RETURN TO ALLAH, regardless of past transgressions; you still have a chance until your last breath.

And NEVER ABANDON SALAH. There are times when we don't feel like praying, or prayer may feel burdensome. But that's okay; it's human nature to feel low. Even if you don't feel like it, JUST SHOW UP on your prayer mat.

Never doubt your Duas and to never feel lonely.

When My servants ask you ˹O Prophet˺ about Me: I am truly near. I respond to one's prayer when they call upon Me. So let them respond ˹with obedience˺ to Me and believe in Me, perhaps they will be guided ˹to the Right Way˺.
Quran - 2:186

"When is the help of Allāh?" Unquestionably, the help of Allāh is near.
Quran - 2:214

Exercise restraint in moments of anger; refrain from actions that may lead to regret, both in this world and the hereafter.

To be content with Allah's Qadr.

After every difficulty comes ease.

Give yourself the opportunity to learn about Islam and you'll not practice anything but Islam.

PRESERVING MEMORIES

The sight of the leap year filled me with wonder, as I pondered Allah's grace in allowing me to share this moment with my beloved ones and to embrace new friendships that have enriched my life. Though the day may appear unremarkable, I felt compelled to capture its essence, finding beauty in the simplicity and gratitude in the presence of cherished companions.

29.02.2024

A day so unique, yet not really special. Documenting today - My day began feeling sleepy; Dad was already awake, sitting on the sofa. I sat beside him, leaning on his broad shoulders, feeling his breath. A weird vibe filled the air with sadness in silence. It was Thursday, and I intended to fast since the week began. Unsure because I missed suhoor, I got ready, doing my skincare routine. Dad called me and gave me fruits; he bought plenty of them the day before and cut them today, handing some to me. I couldn't deny him, so I grabbed a bite. That was my break fast. I reached college, missing the first class as usual. A pretty normal day with classes running all day, teasing and laughing with my bestie. The heat was intense as it's welcoming summer. Made banana, apple milkshake when I reached home. AND! I had a beautiful dream of cherry blossoms. Had lunch, and now I'm strolling on the terrace, chasing sunsets after so long, listening to the Quran. Ramadan is around the corner, on March 11 In Shaa Allah.

    Alhamdulillah, just got done with Maghrib. Sent duas to a few of my friends. My friend Sana just video called me; she was dining out with Farha. Then I scrolled and fell asleep.

Just as I do, I encourage you to do the same. Whether it's your birthday, an anniversary, or simply an ordinary Sunday, take the time to document it. Record every little thing you did that day, every fleeting feeling you experienced, and leave a small reminder for your future self. These moments, both significant and mundane, weave together the tapestry of our lives, offering valuable insights and memories to cherish for years to come.

My Yellows,
If any of you experience harsh behavior from your families or suffer abuse in any way, do not lose hope in the mercy of Allah. You must question and envy others, but remember that Allah chose you to be a part of your household, just as He chose Yusuf [as] to be a part of such a family. Where his own brothers conspired against him, where his only support was his father. He not only fell into their traps but also faced many trials ahead. If someone wrongs you, remind yourself how Yusuf [as] was imprisoned on false accusations for years! And also remind yourself of how Allah blessed Yusuf immensely! Every trial, every pain, every test you go through, our prophets and their families, companions have already gone through that! Look at their life, study them, learn how they handled the situation, learn duas they made, and pray firmly with full trust of it coming true.

I often fall out of words when I listen to my friends' struggles, but the only thing that can give them relief is knowing that Allah doesn't wrong a soul, and Allah doesn't burden a soul more than it can bear. There's surely a greater reward awaiting for you.

Sometimes, running away from your thoughts or fears, or living with guilt and fears, isn't the answer. Eventually, you must sit down and confront them. It doesn't have to happen all at once; start speaking and sorting things out in your mind. You can't always reside within your thoughts, can you? Let things out slowly... I pray you find the courage to release what troubles you and hinders your happiness♡

APPRECIATION

As I got this chance to let my words reach out to the world, I wanna add something more.

I appreciate you, yes, YOU!
I appreciate you for having that intention
I appreciate you to be able to finally decide it
I appreciate you taking baby steps towards it
I appreciate you trying your best
I appreciate you that even when you're about to lose hope, you're still keep going on
I appreciate you for holding on
I appreciate you for all your failures
I appreciate you for all your unsuccessful attempts
I appreciate you for getting up after falling
I appreciate your success, your hardwork behind it
I appreciate you for taking stand for yourself
I appreciate you moving out of your comfort zone
I appreciate you for migrating to different places for studies/work/marriage
I appreciate you for choosing YOU
I appreciate you for all the sacrifices you've made
I appreciate you for working hard to crack that exam
I appreciate you for tackling all the things

I appreciate you for handing over your CV again for your job or for attempting that exam once again
I appreciate you for trying again
I appreciate you for not loosing hope
I appreciate your efforts in your relationship
I appreciate your friendship
I appreciate your existence
I appreciate you for managing all the house chores
I appreciate you for looking over your family
I appreciate you for taking that one tiny step towards your goal
I appreciate you for upbringing of your children
I appreciate you for taking care of others
I appreciating you for putting them first
And also for putting yourself first
I appreciate you for checking up on your friends
I appreciate you for supporting them, and being there for them
I appreciate you for the patience you've endured
I appreciate your courage
I appreciate you for all the things you do to make your relationship work out
I appreciate you for choosing to be kind and gentle with speech

I appreciate you for not harming others
I appreciate you for sorting things out,
I appreciate you for leaving those assumptions and having an actual talk
I appreciate you for taking care of yourself
I appreciate you for loving yourself and others
I appreciate you for taking out time for your family
I appreciate you for always helping others
I appreciate you for your good thoughts
I appreciate you of how you worry about others

I might've missed many things to mention but know that, I appreciate you for EVERYTHING!
And I'm SO PROUD of you ♡

Whenever you feel like you need something to share, or just need someone to listen, just send me an email, although I couldn't be of any help but I can let you feel heard.

CH 07
HOMEBOUND
narratives

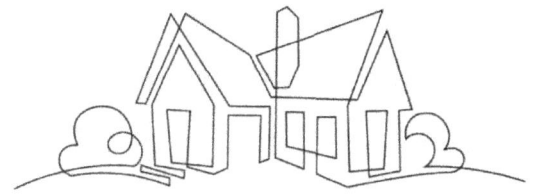

Do this when you're dining with your family
Ask your parents to fill your glass of water, or be seated such that you can ask them water
Cause, ibn-e-Abbas (ra) was asked,
"What form of the charity is best?"
He said, " Giving water to drink."
Prophet Muhammad (pbuh) said:
"Whoever digs a well, no thirsty soul will drink from it whether it be a human, jinn or bird, except that Allah will reward him on the day of Judgement."

So, at the last you're just gifting them rewards

Thanks me later

PRAYER PARTNERS

One of the funniest incidents happened while I was praying with my 1 and a half-year-old niece. Alhamdulillah, she knows a little about namaz. As I said takbeer and folded my hands under my scarf, she observed me and put her hands under her shirt as she was not wearing a scarf.

I couldn't help but smile. Later on, when I raised my shahadat finger, she grabbed it as if to take me somewhere. And during sujood too! She did many more funny things like snatching my scarf, crawling over me during sujood, sitting on my lap, and more!

What's the funniest thing they did with you?

7.11.2022

MOM'S MULTIFUNCTIONAL MOISTURIZER

I've been using a moisturizer, both at home and when leaving the house, which is surprising. It has a thick consistency and is a little sticky, making it difficult to spread. I thought maybe my mom hadn't mixed anything in this one, which is why it's thick. I even wondered if she had added something like phitkedi [I'm not really sure what it is].

Then today, my mom handed me the moisturizer bottle and asked me to put it in the bathroom. I asked, "Why!?" She replied, "Because I stored body wash in it..." I exclaimed, "MUMMMYYYYYYYY...!!!"

Just mom things!
She stores anything in any container.

Everyone laughed!
I was already struggling with pimples, and I applied body wash to my bare face, followed by loose powder... ahh!

22.08.2023

What's the silliest thing your mom has ever done?

SILENT STRUGGLES
A Reflection on Regrets and Helplessness.

I may appear carefree, and I may approach house chores with laziness (though I do them, okay!). I may always seem easygoing, but deep down, I harbor many regrets. I regret not being able to utter 'no' or even nod my head, and it's even harder to do so in real life. Even at this stage, I still wander aimlessly, feeling insecure about everything—what's happening and what's to come. I lack courage and boldness to stand up for myself. I'm not knowledgeable enough to argue, and what's more, I can't even console my father anymore. My heart sinks and my eyes well up whenever I see him stressed. I don't have the words, nor can I bring myself to hug him, pat him, and say, "It's gonna be alright, Daddy," as I used to do. I've become accustomed to this feeling of helplessness.

It's true that we can't feel others' pain, nor can we fully relate or understand them. I realized this when I tried to imagine carrying my father's burdens on my shoulders—I felt as if I would crumble under the weight, yet he stands firm in our eyes, though he might be barely hanging on. And it's true that it's hard to share our worries because he thinks bearing them alone is enough. It's true that sometimes they prefer to be alone in the dark; I knew this when he told me, "Go, go, turn off everything, and leave." Silly me couldn't bring myself to sit with him and just went out. It's true that their back slouches, their head hangs low, and all they can do is put their hands on their foreheads.

My heart breaks when I see him like this. My last chance for the day was to massage his legs, run my fingers through his hair, and kiss his forehead. But when I went to him, for the first time in a while, I saw him snoring, so I didn't want to disturb him even though I knew he might not be sleeping.

Every father might have felt this, and every child might have seen the pain in their eyes. We don't speak of it to our friends or even with our family, so it just keeps weighing us down, and we forget to lift them up during these times.

But I pray that our words, hugs, and duas strengthen them. I pray for all parents to be endlessly happy and free of tensions. Aameen.

As I gently close my diary, I'm struck by the raw honesty of my words. They speak not just of my own experiences, but of the universal struggles we all face in our relationships. We've all felt the weight of regret, the pang of empathy, and the desire to bridge the gap between ourselves and our loved ones.

In these shared moments of vulnerability, I find solace in knowing that I'm not alone. Our journeys may be different, but the emotions we navigate are remarkably similar. So, as you read these pages, may you find echoes of your own experiences and take comfort in the knowledge that we're all in this together.

Until we meet again, may we continue to explore the depths of our hearts and forge connections that sustain us through life's ups and downs.

IMPACT OF CHILDHOOD

Understanding a child's heart can be quite difficult at times.

My nephew, AllahuAkbar, he's so stubborn! He has a habit of bottling up his emotions, and despite our constant reminders, he often chooses to keep them inside, leading to bursts of anger. One day, he stormed upstairs, throwing things around, and when we tried to intervene, he started hitting himself—I was startled. But then, suddenly, he burst into tears. I held him in my arms to calm him down, and after a while, he opened up about missing his mother and shared some of the things that were bothering him. We apologized and brought him downstairs.

During Maghrib, I asked him to join me in prayer, and SubhanAllah, it felt so beautiful as we recited loudly together. I led the prayer, and I couldn't help but think, "Ahhh... This is how boys feel every day, praying in congregation, SubhanAllah." I wished that salah would never end. But the most beautiful part was his dua—it was so heartfelt and inclusive of everything!

But what I've come to realize is that children remember everything they experience, as childhood is a crucial part of their development. As they grow, every sight, sound, and interaction leaves a lasting impact on them for life. Many children suffer from traumas that shape their future.

It's important for us to put ourselves in their shoes, considering the words we choose, our actions, the environment we provide, and the vibes we emit. Everything we do can either positively or negatively affect them. Raising children is one of the most challenging tasks we face.

May Allah bless all parents. Creating a bond where children feel safe to open up, share their feelings, and feel secure is truly an honorable task!

And those who are still wrapped up in their past, traumatized with what happened/ grew in toxic family/went through things in their childhood which they never spoke about even to their parents, I suggest you to have a talk with them, sometimes a good talk solves everything or atleast you'll feel better.

And I pray that you find comfort in Allah's remembrance, I pray you unwrap yourself and let the present shine you, May Allah heal you, Aameen.
8.07.2022

THE PANDEMIC

Today while writing date on my exam booklet, I wrote '22-05-2025' that came out so naturally! But then I was doubtful is it '24' or '25' then I corrected it as 25 doesn't roll off the tongue easily.

And this thought frequently hits me..that we survived the worst pandemic ever! When I look back and recall all those days, a sense of fear instills within me and literally give me chills, like SubhanAllah!! How merciful Allah has been upon us, that He saved me, you, n everyone here, specially our loved ones too, Alhamdulillah!!
[May Allah have mercy on them who passed away and grant their families sabr and strength]

WE LITERALLY SURVIVED IT!!! just recall those scenes, news, lockdow, no entry in kabah...it seems like a worst nightmare to me.

But look at the world now! Everything is resumed, infact it got even more busier than the world was before pandemic, which shows the transient nature of the time and the worldly life!

Let's always be grateful to Allah no matter what situation you're in!

My mini diary,

Today, I noticed something interesting while observing my niece: how swiftly their emotions change! One moment she was laughing, and the next she was crying. I wondered what goes on in their little hearts to cause such rapid shifts in emotions. Surprisingly, I experienced something similar today—I was so happy, but just one piece of news completely altered my mood. And now, I'm back to feeling normal. It's a phenomenon that seems to affect everyone around here. Remember, it's important not to bottle up your emotions, but that doesn't mean you should lash out when you're angry; it hurts too.

Well, that's all for my mini diary. B-bye!

What did you wonder about today?

01.11.2021

FRIDAY CHRONICLES

This is from around 3-4 years ago, I guess. At that time, I became more conscious of Fridays, and since then, they always excited me. Well, my Fridays had a journey too. That was just the beginning, and I used to plan what to wear, what to pray, and what to do. I'd plan my Friday throughout the whole week.

One of my biggest concerns was finding an excuse to skip college, and my college was SO strict [WHAT A JAIL IT WAS]. But Alhamdulillah, I still managed to bunk my Friday afternoon classes, hihi.

Anyways, I was at home, and I cleaned and set up my whole place to pray as the time was ticking near to Jumma prayer. I was hurrying and telling everyone to start Jumma preps. I remember that day vividly.

Even though my nails are usually short, so it wouldn't matter even if I missed a Friday, BUT I was so persistent that I used to cut them even shorter to lessen my sins. And I did all the Jumma things - Surah, Durood, and all! [in the most exciting way]

Then, to my surprise, as I prepared for Jumma, I noticed that no one else seemed to be getting ready. Puzzled, I asked my siblings why they weren't joining in the preparations, only for them to burst into laughter, informing me that it was actually Thursday, not Friday.

Still seated on my prayer mat, I couldn't hold back the flood of tears. Who plays such a prank? I was deeply hurt by their jest, and I spent the entire day in silence, nursing my disappointment. Though it may seem trivial to others, at that moment, the significance of Fridays was profound for me, and no one could truly understand the depth of my feelings.

MY FATHER'S ADVICE

The first thing he said was, "Salah!" Always prioritize your prayers, leave everything upon hearing the call of Allah, and offer namaz without fail.

Moreover, he always, ALWAYS! reminds us to engage in dhikr, regardless of what we're doing at the moment—whether it's university work, household chores, or even using our phones.

Keep your tongue moist with dhikr at all times.

I didn't realize its impact until I immersed myself in constant dhikr; truly, "in the remembrance of Allah do hearts find comfort" (Quran 13:28). I began to find joy in my own company.

Lastly, he always advises us to be content with whatever Allah has blessed us with and to consider those less fortunate than us. As the hadith states:

Abu Hurayrah (may Allah be pleased with him) reported that the Prophet (may Allah's peace and blessings be upon him) said: "Look at those who are below you, and do not look at those who are above you, for that is more likely to hold you back from belittling the blessings that Allah has bestowed upon you."

A DAY WITH THE LITTLE ONES.

What happened was.. something that occurs all too often. They didn't notice me slipping out, even though they were there! Otherwise, I would've had to sneak away secretly, as they always follow me wherever I go. I called my sister, triumphantly declaring, "Mission complete! I didn't fall into their trap." I ventured a little farther, but what did I hear? Them shouting my name with an evil laugh, running down the road toward me.

I felt frustrated. Shouting in the middle of the road, I exclaimed, "Can't you all let me go alone just once? Is it necessary to always cling to me?" I don't even know how to ride a scooter, yet I have to take them on foot, buy them chips, drop them home, and then head to work. All by WALKING! But still, I always do it, making numerous trips from home to the store and back. However, this time it was getting late, and our road lacks streetlights, with huge vehicles passing by.

Now, tell me, how am I supposed to take two children with me? I pleaded with my niece to go home, and I was so furious that I began to cry. I told them, "I'm crying, please go home." At some point, my nephew understood and went back home.

But my niece! Allahu Akbar! She wanted a compass, and despite my assurance that I would bring it later, she insisted, "I need it now, NOW!" This is why they say we should learn from children and make dua—how persistent they are! They cry, rebel, and annoy, but in the end, they make us listen to them. SubhanAllah.

Anyway, circling back to the topic,

As someone with a soft heart, I found myself surrendering in the end—I was genuinely crying! I made a deal with her, "I'll buy you that, but then I'll never talk to you again." She ran back! It seemed like my emotional plea had struck a chord with her, hihi. With a sense of relief, I headed towards an auto. But just as I was about to sit, she came running back again, with an evil laugh.

The frustration I felt at that moment... May Allah have mercy. Nevertheless, I took her to the shop, bought her things, dropped her home, and then headed to work.

Note: All this took 2 hours!

Picture me, shouting at them. On the road, people would probably assume I was either their kidnapper or their mother.

Now, you might think my nephew is a good boy. But no! When he wanted crayons, let me tell you how he tortured me. He dashed onto the main road!!!! My niece chased after him to catch him, and I chased after them both! Quite a spectacle, right?! But wait, there's more. He made me sprint all over the vegetable market. Instead of selling their vegetables, all the vendors were staring at me. He even hid behind an electric pole, trying to evade me, but Alhamdulillah, I caught a glimpse of him, or else I would've been running all over the place in search of him. In short, I took him to the store (crossing the main road with two children). There too, he kept me on my toes, wanting this and that. But eventually, we made it back home safely, Alhamdulillah.

well I've more such stories, will tell you sometime
but for now let's see what the other chapters hold

CH 08
A PALLETE OF
feelings

Does dreams and goals have to be grand?

As I'm still lost, unknown of 'what's best for me', unclear of what to pursue, skeptical of who I'm, I think my dreams aren't grand as others, my goals aren't luxuriant, I guess it's to spread kindness, to radiate my akhlaq, to help others, to build a solid, unbreakable, beautiful relationship with my Rab, to teac others what I've learnt.

But the regrets, the feelings of being left out will forever be burried in my heart, it'll always weigh me down, and it'll continue to haunt me.

I pray and expect the best from You, Ya Allah,
I leave everything upon You, My Rab
Please take care of my imaan, of my heart, of my soul and body, and EVERY concern of my life.

I've a weak heart as well! I get hurt easily too!
I think the same, Even if they say it as a joke,
it hurts. But little things make me happy as well!
And I'm sure it's the same with you too.
Feeling hurt and happy is alot more better than
feeling numb.

WALLS BETWEEN HEARTS

I've noticed that your heart builds walls around it. I can literally feel it. If something in a relationship bothers you and prevents you from opening up, it's likely due to those walls between both hearts.

It's truly painful that you can't penetrate their heart with the wall in between. It pulls back your words, your gestures, into your own heart, not allowing them to pass through the barrier. This hesitation makes you feel as if your love for them is diminishing.

Even after many efforts, you might create a window, but you can never demolish the wall between you and them.

Though the wall may stand, a formidable divide, Love's light still shines, never to be denied. So let us cherish the moments, however small, For love finds a way, to conquer walls, after all.

In the shadow of these walls, let's remember that love is a gentle force, capable of softening even the hardest of barriers. With each tender gesture and heartfelt conversation, we chip away at the defenses that separate us, revealing the boundless affection that lies beneath. So, let's cherish the journey of dismantling these walls, knowing that with each step forward, we draw closer to a love that knows no limits.

BEAUTIFUL TRAP

I've always heard about music addiction, I began thinking how can someone be addicted to it, how come it's so hard on them to overcome it. Until very recently when I was at my cousin's annual function, I sensed that yeah, it's beautiful. Although there were moments when I didn't like such performances but I enjoyed that evening, Astaghfirullah. Allahuakbar the way they beautify sins and make it look marvelous makes it harder to not let ourselves surrender. I tried hard not to love it, or not to get excited but music is such a thing which makes your heart go crazy, the way those songs were playing on super high volume and the disco lights were bright enough to make your eyes close. I then had to leave cuz it was getting late, not gonna lie, but I truly regretted that I left such full of fun environment, Astaghfirullah. But Alhamdulillah, it's better I believe that it's this moment, that if you ain't successful in protecting your nafs from such alluring sins, then it just drags you in the dark pith, where it's difficult to find way out. Alhamdulillah.

EMBRACING LIFE'S RHYTHMS

A Prayer for Joy Today and Tomorrow

I witnessed countless tales, heard many sighs from people trapped in a helpless state, entwined in a never-changing, never-ending cycle. In the eyes of each one, I glimpsed untold stories, resonating with them yet afraid to fully relate. Every conversation with them stirs my fears.

As you navigate your way home, to university, to your workplace, observe the vendors, laborers, and individuals like you, all immersed in the same routine. It frightens me to imagine placing myself in their shoes, to feel what they feel.

This morning, en route to my lecture, the recurring thought enveloped me until I realized that what I'm doing right now is a routine in itself. I don't feel trapped because I breathe it in—I find joy in the process.

Yes, that's the essence! Don't worry about the future; focus on whether you enjoy what you do. Whether it's stitching, pressing clothes, opening a shop daily, sitting at your desk, teaching all day, or nurturing children. Even if it's an inescapable routine, it becomes bearable when we find joy in it or, at the very least, avoid suffocating ourselves.

That's how a new dua was added to my list,
"Ya Allah, I don't know what future holds for me,
or what cycle I would be pedaling on, but let me find myself happy doing it, and reward it for me,
I don't know if I'll be a working woman or a homemaker or both...whatever it is,
Let me enjoy and find happiness in it.
Let me be happy in serving my family,
in taking care of them, in raising my kids,
in waking up before anyone else,
making breakfast and packing their lunch,
in supporting and looking after my other half,
in all the responsibilities I'll be handed over,
as the queen of the house.

And don't ever let me feel trapped, and suffocated,
And don't ever let me feel worthless,
And don't ever let me sigh in a helpless state,
And let me pause and rest every now and then,
And energies me to do my best in anything I choose.

Aameen Ya Rabbul A'alameen.

NIGHTTIME RIDDLES
Echoes of Uncertainty.

Something keeps me awake,
Silent thoughts,
unnamed and strange,
feelings unknown, a numb embrace,
closing my eyes seems an odd chase.

Group chat notifications hum in my phone,
Yet, I can't muster the will to pick it up.
Staring at these walls and the whirring fan,
I ponder what's absent, what overflows,
What's right, what's wrong,
And what my present harbors,
Will I cherish it or wish for its demise.

But fear not, for within this silent night,
Lies the promise of dawn's gentle light,
In every question, in every sigh,
There's a whisper of hope, soaring high.

So let us embrace the uncertainty,
For within it lies our true destiny,
With each breath, with each rise,
We'll find the courage to claim our prize.

1:39am

WORN OUT IN UNFURLING
The Dilemma of Social Weariness

Want to cut off from everything
Away from the world
I'm tired of unfurling,
Want to go back to being furled.
Safe and secure;
Lost and unknown..
I'm tired of checking on people.
tired of being there for them.
tired to keep them entertained.
tired of forcing conversations.
tired of making efforts.

But I can't just leave them all,
What if my one question 'are you okay?'
Might make someone feel good..
This mere thought is keeping me up

And know that it's okay to feel worn out from the demands of social interaction. Taking time for yourself doesn't mean abandoning others entirely. Remember, even small gestures like asking someone if they're okay can make a big difference. Taking care of yourself allows you to be there for others in a more meaningful way. Take a breath, recharge, and remember that your well-being matters too.

SURRENDERING TO SERENITY

A Prayer for Confidence and a Regret-Free Journey

Ya Allah, why is it so hard to calm my heart, or to strengthen my heart for the upcoming challenges, Ya Allah, why am I so backward, coward, weak, and lack confidence.
Ya Allah, why is it that I don't know what I'm supposed to do, am I bound to have regrets? forever in my life?
Or do I make things harder than they actually are? I don't know, my Rab, I'm so nervous and afraid of what future holds for me, I wish, atleast, it doesn't hold any regrets, In Shaa Allah. Oh Allah, Oh my Rab, Oh my Creator, Oh The All Knowing, make my affairs easy for me, put khair in it, put your blessings in it, I'm leaving all my worries upon you, I know You, My Rab will do what's best for me, I expect the best from You, Ya Allah, make my both lives easier, make my end well, aameen.

From now, whenever I'm afraid and worried about my future, I'll turn them into positive thoughts and expect the best from You, cause You are what we think of You.

As we journey through life's ups and downs, it's natural to feel overwhelmed at times. But in those moments, remember to surrender your worries to a higher power, to Allah. Let go of the weight of the past and embrace the power of positivity. Turn your challenges into opportunities for growth and trust in Allah's guidance. By focusing on the positive and placing our trust in Him, we can find strength, peace, and endless possibilities. So, let's all strive to turn our negatives into positives and have faith that the best is yet to come, guided by the wisdom and grace of Allah.

THE KEY TO LASTING RELATIONSHIPS.

The strongest pillar upon which a relationship rests is respect, even before love. Relationships are delicate yet strong; they can be your weakness and strength, lagging you down or pushing you up. A relationship must go through all phases to stand strong and become deep, but the only constant variable throughout the whole course is respect—a pillar so strong yet so fragile. A little crack and it collapses. Make sure to nurture it with love, fun, understanding, trust and appreciation.

Respecting their individual lives, their thinking and points of view, things close to them, their decisions, and their reasons is crucial. It's this respect that fortifies the foundation of any relationship, ensuring its strength and endurance.

ENVY

Just because you envy something, doesn't mean you're unhappy, jealous, or ungrateful. It's natural to feel a pang of longing, but let's channel that emotion into something beautiful. Let it remind us to cherish what we have and strive for our own dreams. Keep checking your intentions and ensure they're pure. Instead of harboring negativity, let envy inspire empathy and goodwill towards others. Wish them the best, for the energy we put out into the world has a way of coming back to us, enriching our lives in unexpected ways.

FORGIVING FEARS

A Letter to My Future Self with Understanding

I wrote this in my diary, and it feels consoling, so I hope it may console you as well.

"I know I'll regret this moment in the future. But, dear future me, I won't blame her. At that time, she was burdened with a lot of fears and insecurities, which may seem trivial to you now. Please don't blame her for not overcoming her fears. Please try to understand her."

SEEING BEYOND
The Heart's Perception of True Values

It is with the heart that one can truly perceive; what is essential often escapes the eye. I believe wealth is materialistic; now, material possessions hold little value to me. It's about trust, family, friends, and my support system—things that resonate deeply within, visible to the heart rather than the eyes.

In the tapestry of life, let us weave threads of love, trust, and companionship, for these are the true treasures that enrich our souls and illuminate our journey.

REFLECTIONS ON FAITH

To be candid, I find myself pondering the depths of love and its true essence. How can one love another so profoundly, willing to sacrifice everything?

Let's shift our focus from worldly relationships and delve into our love for Prophet Muhammad (peace be upon him).

We often proclaim our love, but do we truly comprehend its magnitude?

My Arabic teacher once posed a thought-provoking question: "How much do you love your parents?" "Beyond measure!" we fervently replied. "Now, imagine you're married. Your love for your spouse surpasses that for your parents. And when you have children, your love for them eclipses all."

But then, hr challenged us further: "Your love should transcend even that of your children."

This reflection left me contemplating the boundless nature of love and its significance in our lives.

That's when I finally understood the significance of the hadith narrated by Anas:

"The Prophet (peace be upon him) said, 'None of you will have faith till he loves me more than his father, his children, and all mankind.'"

This hadith resonated deeply with me, especially as I reflected on the story of Eid ul Adha.

I've often heard nasheeds and duas where people express the sentiment, "May my father be sacrificed for you," which always struck me profoundly.

Now, at a stage where I deeply cherish my parents and fear losing them, the notion of being willing to sacrifice them for the love of the Prophet (peace be upon him) has stayed with me since my teacher posed that question and shared that example.

It's a reminder for me to strive towards strengthening my faith and nurturing my imaan. May Allah grant us all the strength to preserve and enhance our faith, and may He increase our imaan to the fullest. Aameen.

Ref: Sahih al-Bukhari 15 Book 2, Hadith 8

EXPECT THE GREATEST REWARD FOR YOUR DEEDS!

This is one of my wishes from my bucket list – to remove every stone from the path, making it easier for others to walk. I cherish this deed not only for its intrinsic value but also because it aligns with a Sunnah. Every time I encounter a small obstacle be it a little branch or a stone, I can't move on until I've cleared it away. With each act, I hope to please my Rab, anticipating that just as I strive to make paths clean, He will remove obstacles from my own life."

Similarly, sleeping on the right side!
Whenever I lay down, I lay on my left side, which is the most comfortable posture for me, but I just can't sleep! Cause it's sunnah to sleep on the right.

I then turn to right and expect it to be my ticket to jannah! YEAH! I expect Jannah through this little deed cause

Allah says: 'I am just as My slave thinks I am..' Expect goodness, always, from Allah.

[no matter how small the deed is, do it only to please Allah]

A STEP TOWARDS HIM

I rode pillion behind my father on his bike on my way to college. I was thinking, 'Allah, please keep my parents safe,' and then this thought occurred to me: 'I am such a sinner, how does Allah even listen to me?' Then I recalled an incident when I was upset with my nephew and acting tough I told him, 'I'm not going to talk to you'. When my niece said, 'I think you need to apologize to him, he seems sad,' I replied, 'Why would I? It's his fault!' But when I saw his eyes, when I felt his silence, my heart melted. I could no longer stay upset with him; I called him and fed him with my own hands. I was like, 'YEAHHHH, THAT'S HOW ALLAH FEELS!!' when we turn back to Him! It's all a step closer, a step towards Him.

EMBRACING VULNERABILITY :
The Beauty of Feeling

There was a fleeting moment where I wished for my heart to be void of emotions, any kind of feelings. That fleeting moment felt lasting, where I wished to care less, love less, worry less, and ultimately to become numb, feeling nothing.

But I was afraid of this plea to be answered, because I couldn't imagine how barren, lifeless, and hard my heart would be.

This made me realize, and I was grateful for every pang of emotion I feel. Yes, there are moments when things get overwhelming, and you're confused about what you truly feel or get drained. All we need to do is control what we feel and know who truly is worthy of our emotions. Also, know that to treat every stranger with kindness and smiles."

ECHOES OF THE SOUL

Navigating the Labyrinth Within

In the labyrinth of self, where shadows roam, The heart's whispers echo, seeking home, A symphony of doubts, a tangled thread, In the depths of the soul, where truth is led.

"I loathe myself, yet love's embrace I find, In a world of cruelty, sweetness intertwined. Cruelty in my veins, yet sweetness in their eyes, A contradiction within, where truth lies. In the mask I wear, in the shadow's cast, Why cling to illusions of the past? Yearning to vanish, to fade away, Yet fearing the heartache I may convey."

Amidst the labyrinth of self and soul, Where echoes of doubt and questions roll, Remember, dear heart, your worth unseen, In the eyes of those whose love convenes. Though shadows loom and doubts may rise, Know your light shines beyond disguise. For in the heart's silent symphony, Lies the truth of our shared humanity.

EMBRACING TEARS:
The Strength in Vulnerability

I express every emotion of mine with tears—happiness, sadness, fury, confusion, feeling stuck, or lost. Sometimes, I hate it because it's mistaken for weakness, yet being sensitive isn't something I choose. Crying instead of getting angry doesn't signify weakness; it's merely my natural response to the situation.

Despite this, I feel a sense of pride in my ability to express emotions openly. It demonstrates the sincerity and depth of my feelings.

In a world that often equates vulnerability with weakness, it takes courage to wear your heart on your sleeve. Let your tears be a testament to your strength, a reminder of your humanity. Embrace your emotions, for they are the threads that weave the fabric of your existence, imbuing it with depth and richness.

CH 09
JAZBAAT
e – urdu

Har ladki ki kahani

Kya ajeeb si zindagi hai,
Chand saal me sab badal jaega,
Meri pehchan, mera maqsad, meri zimmedari, mera darja, meri jagah, Mera ghar, mera pariwaar, sab kuch,
Parai hojaungi mai, vidai hogi meri,
Fir apne hi ghar aane ijazath leni hogi
Apne hi ghar me rukne mohlat maangni hogi
Apne hi ghar jane bahane dhunne honge
Kya beetegi dil pe mere
Jab sunungi ki "wo tumhara ghar na raha abse ye tumhara ghar hai"
Jis dehlees pe baith Kar baba ka intezaar karti thi,
Baba keh kar, haath tham kar andar jati thi,
Ab usi dehleez se haath chor kar alwida kehna hoga
Jis dehleez se bijijhak aati jaati thi,
Ab usi dehleez ko paar karne darwaza khat khatana hoga
Jab ghar se zyada der bahar reh jati to call aata tha ki "Ghar aane ka irada hai b ya nahi?"
Ab wahi Ghar wale puchenge "Kab jare ho?"
Jab doston k yaha thori der k liye chale gai to, log bolte the ki mat bheja karo use,
Ab wahi log kahenge ki kitne din rakh loge.

Kya silsila hai zindagi ka,
Jis Maa k hath k khane ki adat thi
Ab usi Maa k khane ko taras jaungi.
Jab "assignment projects ki deadlines me phasi hoti" aur ab "aj to ye paka liya, ab Kal kya pakaun" zyada pareshan karegi
Jis darwaze ko hamesha khula dekha,
Ab usi darwaze se muh pherna padhega
Jab din bhar bas padhai karte ya bas sote hue phone use kar k bhook lag jati thi
Ab saare ghar ko khila kar bhook mit jaaegi
Jis Ghar k Har kone pe haq jatati thi ab usi Ghar ki cheez istemal karne sonchna hoga,
Jis Ghar me Har cheez lad Kar leti thi,
Ab usi Ghar se kuch lene me dil khatakta hai.

Jis ghar ka saara kharcha mujh par hota tha, ab usi ghar ka ek rupiya b qarz lagta hai.
Jis ghar me bachpan se rehti aai hun, ab us ghar ki har diwaar anjaan bane honge.
Kya haal hoga mere dill ka
jab jis ghar par me haq jamati thi, ab mera na rahega..
Jin ghar walon k khilaf ek lafz sunne ki bardash nahi thi,
Ab unhi k kehne par chup hona padra hai.

Dil tut jata hai baba se ye sun kar ki "beti ho, sari zindagi to nai bitha sakunga ghar par"
Betiyan rehmat zarur hai lekin shayad is rehmat ka bhoj b utna hi hoga
 tabhi to ruksat karne k baad kehte hain, "ek ka to kaam hogaya, Ab bas dusri ka hojae fir sukuun hai"
Samajhti hun ki ye tumhara farz hai, zimmedari hai, par kya karun, dard to hota hai.

Kya ajeeb se zindagi hai,
is haqeeqat ko apnaane,
saari zindagi lag jaegi.

Maqsadh, khwab

Bachpan me jab kisi ne bhi mujh se mera khwab pucha, mera bas bakhi bachiyon ki tarah ek hi lafz nikalta tha, 'doctor'
Bachpan me khel b khelin to sirf teacher teacher aur doctor doctor khelin hai
Par kya pata tha ki ye lafz itne halke nahi,

Jab school ka akhri saal chal raha tha,
Tab mere bhot se khwab the ki, kisi ku kuch to kisi ku kuch kehti thi,
Scientist, doctor, pilot, police, prime minister, environmentalist tobah, aur bhi bhot se khwabein the.

Kya pata tha ki khwab ki talash me niklun to yun kho si jaungi, ki jaha madad karne log to honge lekin kis ka haath thamun, aur kis par itebaar karun, samajh nahi aaega.

Aur kya pata tha ki khwab dhunne itne saal lag jaenge, ki haqiqat me rehna bhul jaenge.
Kya pata tha ki mera ye jo khwab hai, jis ki talash me mai nikli hun uski mol mere anmol waqt se kiya jaega,

Is safar ne bhot kuch sikhaya, kahii logon se milaya, kuch meri tarah talash me the, to kuch apne khwabon ko hasil karne me the.

Aur mai tab bhi unko dekhti thi, aisa lagta tha k khwab paalna b khazana hai
Fir mene bhi apni talash ko bhool kar un logon k khwab k peeche bhaagne lagi
Lekin bas farq itna tha ki, un me wo jazba, wo lagan thi jo mujh me nahi thi

Mujh se puchoge to, mere pas ab bhi koi jawab nahi hoga, me to bas khali hath lauti hun, shayad abhi b puri tarah se nahi lauti hun, mera ek hissa isi talash me phir raha hai..

Jis liye wo phir raha hai,
Jis maqsad ki talash me,
jis khwab ki talash me,
Jis k liye na jaane kitni raatein rone me guzri,
Aur kitne din logon se nazre chupane me..
Kya pata tha ki itne arse ki talash bas is jumle me mojood tha

"Aur mene jinnat aur insaan ko sirf isliye paida kiya taake wo Meri ibadat kare"

Mera maqsad to mere paida hone se pehle hi tai kardiya gaya tha mujh se hi bas pehchanne me gaflat hogai.

Mera maqsad to mere paida hone se pehle hi tai kardiya gaya tha mujh se hi bas pehchanne me gaflat hogai.

Aisa maqsad, aisa khwab jo na hi use me hasil karungi aur na hi pura kyun ki ye meri zindagi k akhri saans tak kayam rahega,

Bakhi log k khwab...wo mehnat karenge aur kisi na kisi din hasil kar hi lenge,
fir wo tamanna, wo tadap, wo mehnat, wo bechain dil, wo lambi raatein, wo qurbaniyan sabhi khatm ho jaengi,

Lekin ek momeen ka dill hamesha apne Rab ko raazi karne me lagega, wahi uska maqsad, aur wahi uska khwab hoga.

Bas ab is dil ko yahi aayat yaad dila dila kar tasalli deni hogi, ki waqai me, mere khwab sab se uumda hai, ki mai waqai me khazane ki haqdaar ban chuki hun mai.

Safar

Zindagi k alag alag modh par khade ham
par safar ek sath ka tha,
Kash Safar lamba hota,
to baatein aur thi karne ko,
Kash manzil dur rehti,
ehsaasat aur the izhar karne ko,
Par manzil aa pahunchi,
fir kabhi milenge,
is baar zindagi k kisi ek modh par.

Izzat - Zevar

Izzath ek esa zevar hai,
jise kamana asaan nahi;
Izzath ek esa zevar hai
jo jajti bohot hai lekin
Agar tut jae to, wo
kisi pathar se kam nahi.
Izzath ek esa zevar hai
jise ham paana to chahte hain,
lekin jab dene ki baari aati hai
kuch hich kichate hai,
toh kuch Bejijagh dete hain.

[my very first urdu writing]

Qubooliyath

Qubooliyath me
Apni Haar aur auron ki jeet ki qubool,
Zindagi me apne kirdaar ko,
apni qadr ko jo Allah ne likhi hai,
zindagi k nizaam ko,
apne kamzor hone ki qubooloyath,
taake tum logon ki himayat qubool kar sako,
Apni achaiyon k sath buraiyon ki qubooliyath
Apne sath apne aage walon k huquuq ki qubooliyath,
Apni aur dusron ki fitrat ki qubooliyath,
Is baat per qubool karna ki jo mere qadr me hai wo mujhe mil Kar hi rahega, Aur jo nahi wo saari kaayanat b mil Kar nahi de sakti.
Jab tum waqai me sab qubool karo na,
To yaqeenan apne dil ko sukuun me paoge.

Aansu

Allah ne shayad aansu ek zaria banaya hai
Taake log apni Khushi aur gham
izhaar kar sake.
Taake jab lafz bayan na kar payen to ye
aansu kaam aajae.
Lekin aansu to bas zaria hi hai,
Kuch gham aansu se b bayan nai ki jaati
Aur na hi alfaaz, us gham k sath jeena ya
bhulana sirf khuda k ekhtiyaar me hai,
jisme us aazmaish me dala hai.
Us pal ruhaani tahammul isi jaanne me hai ki
Allah apne bando ko uski bardash se zyada
bhojh nahi dalta.
Insaano ki sahaaliyat to bas unk gale lagne
me hai.

Aazmaish

sab k Ankhon me takleef thi ek dusre k liye. Har koi apne apne gham aur takleef k sath jeeta hai,
Isme koi kisi ka mukaabla nahi, sab pareshan hai, sab bebas hai apni haalaton par, isme koi farq nahi.
Har koi kahega ki tum par wo nahi beetri jo mujh par beetri hai, lekin haqeeqat to ye hai ki, koi kisi ki takleef nahi jaan sakta aur na hi bardash kar sakta, kyun ki Allah ne Har Bande ko uski quwwat aur Himmat k mutabiq wo aazmaish, wo aziyath di hai.
Isme bas, ek dusre ka sath hone ka ehsaas chahiye, ek dusre ko samajhne ki salahiyath, aur ek dusre ko akela mehsus na hone Dena. Is cheez se to Har shaks ko akela hi guzarna hai, Zahir si baat hai ki Bande ko akelapan mehsus hoga, chahe Usk sath koi ho ya na. Lekin, Jo shaks tumhare sath hai, use bhi akelapan mehsus hota hai tumhe sambhalte sambhalte, tumhe samajhte samajhte...unko bhi Himmat ki zarurat hoti hai taake wo uth sake aur tumhara Sahara ban sake.

Isliye bas ye jaan lo k kuch b ho, tumhe tumhare sabr ka ajr zarur milega, aur tumhe tumhari hisse k saari khushiyan zarur naseeb hogi chahe use aane kitni hi der kyun na hojae, wo tumhare darwaze par zarur dastak degi, kyun ki ye tere Rab ka waada hai –

"Beshak mushikaat k baad aasani hai"
Surah Ash-Sharh

Na'imath

Akele ho to b na'imath,
Kisi k sath ho tab bhi na'imath;
Masroof ho to na'imath,
Bekar ho tab bhi na'imath;
Khush ho to na'imath,
Udaas ho tab bhi na'imath;
Rizq me barkat ho to na'imath,
Rizq me tangi ho tab bhi na'imath;
Befikr ho to na'imath,
Pareshan haal ho tab bhi na'imath;
Jeet mili to na'imath,
Haar mili tab bhi na'imath;
Sehethmand ho to na'imath,
Bimar ho tab bhi na'imath;
Rangeen badal na'imath hai To
Kaale badal bhi!
Subha ki roshni na'imath hai,
To raat ki andheri bhi na'imath hai!
Aise kahi cheezein hai jo
me shayad kabi tasawwur b na kar paun..

na'imath - blessing

Lekin ye zarur pata hai ki
Zindagi khud ek na'imath hai
Jisme har eent Allah k na'imaton se bana hai.
Jiski buniyad hi ek naymat ho
Bas samajhne ki salahiyat chahiye,
Aur fir bande ki apni apni nazariye ki baat hai
Chaho to..
Sab kuch hasil kar k b khud ko itminaam na paao,
Ya kangal reh kar b sukuun me ho.
Bas shukr ka khel hai,
jitne shukrguzar banoge
Utna apne na'imaton me izafa paoge
Zindagi sabki haseen hoti
Bas nazariye ki baat hai..
ye samajhlein ki Allah insaaf karne wala hai,
aur Wo kisi k sath nainsaafi nahi karta.
Apni qadr par sawal nahi, dua kar, ay Bande!

Wese to jaanti hun ki utna asaan nahi hai,
Rab ki Raza me razi hona
Ye bhi ek tareeqa hai Allah k aazmane ka..
Isliye kisi ko kusurwar nahi khada sakti
jab wo ape takleefon se khafa ho
jab wo sawal kare ki, "me hi kyun?"

Apne ap ko yaad dilao, ki tum musalman ho,
Jiska matlab hai, ki tum Allah k har ehkaam par imaan late ho,
chahe wo tumhari samajh me aae ya na aae,
Kyun ki ham nahi jaante jo Wo jaanta hai.

Aur fir apne ap ko ye bhi yaad dilao k,
Allah sattar maa'on se zyada pyar karne wala hai,
Kya Wo Apne bande ko zyada der takleef me rakh sakta hai? Bina kisi ajr k?

Ye bhi yaad dilao k, Allah jisko jitna pasand kare,
Wo use utna hi Aazmaata hai, jese Usne Apne Nabi sallalahu alaihi wa sallam ko kiya tha.

Ye bhi yaad dilao k, tumhare dua ki qubooliyath me isliye deri ho rahi hai kyun ki, tumhara pukarna Use pasand hai.

Fir shayad dil ko thora sukuun mile, apne dil ko hamesha Allah ki yaad me masroof rakhna, fir har mushkil manzil paar kar jaoge.

"Apne andherepan par udaas mat hona
Kyun ki aksar ankhein roshni me bandh hoti hai,
aur andhere me khulti hain.
Jo cheezein tumhe roshni na dikh saki..
wo tumhe andheri dikhati hai"

wese chahun to aur b likh sakti hun lekin suna hai ki..
'samanhdhar ko ishara kaafi hai'

Maa

Meri ammi, dil tham jata hai jab kuch likhne jaun, Mere dil me jo izzat o mohobbat hai kis tarah is alfaaz me bayan karun, mene kaafi waqt guzara sonchne me k kya likhun Maa k bare me, kyun ki me jaanti hun ki aisi koi tehreer nahi jo mukammal hoke b teri wajood ki ehmiyath bayan kar sake. Pata nahi ki kabi is ehsaan ko chuka paungi ya nahi jo tu ne mujhe nau nahine sambhala aur is duniya me laya.

Me to paida hi tujh ko takleef dete hui hun, jis takleef ki shifa bas mere neik amaal aur qidmat se hogi. Sach kehte hai Maa aulaad ki pehli ustadh hoti hai, jisne hame chalna sikhaya, baat karna sikhaya, khane ka adab sikhaya, padhna, likhna sikhaya, har cheez me Maa tera hath hai. Jab dar laga to muh se Maa nikla, Jab dard hua to muh se sirf Maa nikla, kis tarah Teri dua Har Bala k aade aajati hai, aur har Khushi ka zaria. Kis tarah tu apni saari neendein haram karti thi hamare liye, aur fir saara din hamare peeche hi bhag daur karti thi. Tere is baygarz ka ehsaan kis tarah chukaun me?

Tera aas paas rehna, Teri Payal ki awaz, tere hone ka mehsus dil ko itminaam deta hai, tere bina zindagi ko jeena tasawwur b nahi karsakti mai, maa. Waqt kis tarah guzar gaya, hamare peeche Teri saari zindagi chale gai, ab jab me chahun to b Tera guzra hua waqt na lauta paun. Tere kahi ehsaan hai jis ka ehsaas hai mujhe, jese hamare peeche bhagte bhagte, tere pair ka kamzor hona, jese hame utha kar Kamar me dard hona, aur na jane kitne baar ham ne ro kar, tang kar kar sataya hoga tujhe. Zindagi ki tijarat me mahinga sauda kiya, mujhe chuna apne apne khwabon aur azaadi ki keemat par. Ye sab jaante hue bhi me nakaam hojati hun apne hi laailmi ki wajah se.

Kya khoob misaal di hai Rab ne...
Teri mohobbat ki misaal to Allah ne khud di hai,
Usk rehmat ka tasawwur, teri rehmat se ki jati hai

Daant ti ho, ruth ti ho, lekin akhir me, maaf kar hi deti ho. Saari duniya chahe mujh se muh modh le, lekin teri anchal me, mai hamesha apne ap ku paaun.

Aur meri Maa, mai karlungi wo kaam jo tune kaha hai karne ko, aur logon k samne ye ankhon se baatein karna, ankhon se ishare karna kab band karogiii, kyun? koi kuch bolega kya??

Har cheez jaanti ho, Jo b kho jae, chutkiyon me dhun leti ho, agar kohinoor b kho jae, jab b kahogi ki.."dekho wahi to hai"
Is 'wahi' ka nakhsha to tu hi behtar jaane.

Har masle ka hal, Har marz ki dawa tere us youtube channel par mojudh hota hai. Lekin meri Maa, bas teri dua chahiyeee youtube channels ki links nahi!

Sonch rahi hun ki, ab tujh se khana banana seekh hi lena padhega, kyun ki tujh jesa swadh duniya k kisi hath me nahi...Fir chahe usk liye teri itni nok jhok hi sunni padhe

Man karta hai tere hath ko hamesha chumte rahun, tujh se zorrr se gale lagaun. Kese izhaar karun ki mujhe teri kitni qadr hai, Haan jaanti hun ki thori aalsi hun, kitchen me hath nahi batati zyada lekin iska ye matlab nahi ki mujhe teri parwah nahi

Shayad kabi itni parwah na kar sakun jese tu bachpan se mere liye karti aai ho
Allah se bas ye dua hai ki, mujhe itna sabr aur quwwat ataa kare
Ki me tera sahara ban sakun.
Maa jesi meri dhaal hai, dua karti hun ki me bhi tere liye dhaal banun.

Aur Maa, jaanti hun, Mere sath tera bhi waqt guzar raha hai, jese tune mere peeche apni saari zindagi lagai hai, mai bhi apni saari zindagi teri qidmat me guzardun, Allah ye mokha mujh se kabi na cheene.

Hamesha shukrguzar rahungi Allah ka, jisne mujhe itni ek dost se, ek ustadh se, ek sathi se, ek sahare se, nawaza hai jo meri Maa k shakl me hai.

Me bayan karna chordun to ye matlab nahi k mere pas alfaaz nahi bache, balki itni hai ki..mai bayan karte karte sajde me gir padun, Rab ka Shukr adaa karne ki Usne tujhe meri Maa banaya hai.

Baba

Babaaa kya kya likhun me apk bare me?
Itnaaa hai ki.. alfaz kam pad jaenge
Aur shuru kidhar se karun!?
Me jab bhi apk bare me sonchti hun to ankhein nam hojati hai, dil bechain hojata hai, ki ap kab ghar aaoge aur me kab apse gale milun
Bhot dil karta hai ki apse gale milun aur kabi juda na hun..
Lekin utna hi apse gale milne sharm bhi aati hai
Apse ye izhaar karne ki me duniya me sab se zyada me ap hi ko chahti hun.

Jab choti thi to ap hi ne sabse pehle mujhe apnaya, mujhe apna naam diya. Waqai me faqar mehsus karti hun jabi b mere dost mujhe apk naam se bulate hain, itni bulandi mehsus karti hun apne naame me, kyun ki apne jo apni saari zindagi me izzat kamai hai, uska ek hissa lekar chalti hun mai, baba.

Lekin apka naam zuban se lene itni hichkichat hoti hai, me kese apka naam le lun jab mere dil me apka itna ehteraam? Haan wo to alag baat thi.. jab bachpan me, ap se mazak karti thi, jab apk dost banne ki natak karti thi, bhari awaz me apka naam pukarti thi aur ap jaante hue bhi bhage bhage chale aate the..

Wese to mujhe yaad nahi..lekin shayad, me bhi un kahawaton ki tarah.. apki ungli pakad kar chalna seekhi hungi, bachpan to khair chodo Lekin kuch waqt pehle, jab ham hath pakad kar chal rahe the, tab mujhe mehsus hua ki 'Haan shayad bachpan me aise laga hoga mujhe'

Shayad Allah ne apk hathon me shifa rakhi hai, kyun ki me jab bhi bimar huin hun to sirf apka hath maathe par chahiye, jo meri saari takleef ko namm kar deti hai.

Apk haath ka jo ehsaas hai, wo shayad me kabi na bhulun, aisa lagta hai ki mere pas saari kaayanaat hai, ki me duniya ki sabsee raees shaks hun.

Ab bhi yaad hai mujhe wo pal jab ham subah uth kar Fajr padhte the,
Ab bhi yaad hai mujhe wo pal jab ap mujhe apne kandhon par sair karwate the,

Ab bhi yaad hai wo pal jab ap mujhe 'Jokka pada', bulate the/hain

Ab bhi yaad hai jese me apk pas rote hue aai thi ki Mera exam Acha nahi gaya aur ap kehte the "isme rone wali kya baat hai, fail ho, fir wahi class me baitho aur name dost banao"

Apk pair dabana ka, apka sar malish karna ka mokha milna, bhot badi naymath hai mere liye. Apk sath ki Har yaad mere liye bohot azeez hai. Darwaze par apka intezar karna, apki gaadi awaz sun kar pehchan Lena, apk liye darwaza kholna, naymat hai, tohfa hai mere liye.

Khud ko khamosh paati hun, jab ap apne do hath aage kar kar kehte ho ki 'aao ab baitho mere godh me jese bachpan me baith ti thi", "aao kaandhe pe baitho pehle ki tarah"
Waqt kese guzar gaya hai na baba..
Meri tarah shayad ap bhi beeta hua kal yaad karte ho.

Kese ap mere dil ki har baat jaan lete ho, ye tak k mujhe apka wo ek niwala chahiye, Ya wo ek gosht ka tukda jis par meri nazar thi.

Maa ne itni takleef se paida kiya
To apne kahi zyada takleef se mujhe is haal me rakha
Jo mangu uska das gunah zyada la kar diya hai,
Jo chaha use mere hathon me laa samaya hai,
Duniya ki har manzil, har mushkil, har aamaish asaan dikhti hai, jab sath apka ho.
Allah k baad ap hi k wajood se himmat milti hai, mehfooz mehsus karti hun jo shayad hi kisi aur k sath hogi.

Apk bayan se pehle, me apki ache suluuk se hi sikhi hun har cheez.
Ap misaal ho un saari achaiyon ki jo bakhi hai is duniya me.

Jab ap apne hath mathe par rakhte ho, pareshan aur khamoosh baith te ho, to khud ko bebas paati hun aur kehti hun ki 'Kash me ladka hota' taake apki madad kar sakun, fir apne dill ko khud hi dilasa deti hun ki, apki madad Allah khud karega

Dua karti hun ki me apka sahara banu,
jis tarah aapne mujhe har kadam par apna sath diya hai, mera sahara bana hai.

Maa ne nau mahine sabar se mera bhoj uthaya to apne bhi sabar se meri har khwaish ko puri ki,
Kese mujhe ab tak bhi college chorte ho aur kese waqt se pehle lene aajate ho,
Kese mere bas ek kehne par tayar hojate ho,
Chahe safar kaha ka b ho aur kis waqt ka b ho.

Kis tarah ap apni thakaan ko chupate ho,
Apni takleef ko izhaar nahi karte,
Apna dukh, dard, sab ghar k dastak par chod kar aate ho,

Lekin apki ankhein sab kuch bayan kar deti hai,
Apki awaz ki jhalak se, apki chalan se, apk rawaaiyye se, sab pata chal jata hai.

Kabi kabaar puch leti hun ki kya masla hai, lekin zyada tar jab bhi apko pareshan dekhun to, Allah se ap ki hi guftagu karti hun, Usse naraz hoti hun lekin fir Usk wo wade pe yaqeen b karti hun ki Wo apki madad zarur karega, kyun ki jab beti paida hoti hai to Allah ne kaha ki 'jao, me tere baap ki madad karunga'

Mera bas chale to me apki saari pareshnaiya apne kandhon par lelun, lekin jab tasawwur karna shuru kiya to, ghutan mehsus hone lagi, aur me ro padi, ki ap kis tarah sambhalte ho sab kuch baba..

Jis b haal me ho, kitni b thakan kyun na ho, apka wo call zarur aata hai, jisme puchte ho ki, 'muumy se pucho aane se pehle kya lekar aaun'

Ap jese hamare ghar ki mazbooth pahad ho,
Jo ghar ko bikharne se mehfooz rakhti hai.

Maa ki aanchal me pali hun apk saaye me kheli hun, baba..
Allah kare ki ap dono ka saya hameshaa mujh par rahe. Allah bhot bada mehrbaan hai Jisne aplog ko mere liye rehmat bana kar bheja hai.

Aplog ki sikhai hui Har cheez
mujhe sirf Apne Rab k khareeb ki hai..

Na jane kitne aansu bahai hun mai ye likhte waqt..
Par mere alfaaz khatam hone ka naam nahi lere..
...Bas ap dono ki hamesha shukr guzaar rahungi.
Kahi baar ye sawal zubaan tak aaya hai ki puchun
"kya ap mujh se raazi ho"
Lekin fir jawab sunne ki himmat b nahi..

Isliye meri dua me sab se pehla hissa yahi hai k
"mere maa baap aur Mera Rab mujh se raazi hojae"

As our swinging adventure concludes, it's not goodbye but 'see you later' in life's grand amusement park. Until we meet again, may joy fill your days, and may your future chapters be as enchanting as our shared journey!

My yellowsss,
I Love you for Allah's sake♡

EPILOGUE

Dear kindred spirits,

As we bid adieu to these tales, a subtle hue of nostalgia tints the pages—a reflection of the stories that unfurled and the dreams yet to be chased. Before you close this book, let me share a secret desire that dances at the edge of my hopes.

Throughout these verses, I often concluded with the wistful wish of spotting a rainbow—a promise I've missed in the midst of life's hustle. Today, I extend that wish into the open pages of tomorrow, hoping that each of you, dear readers, encounters rainbows after your storms. May vibrant arcs paint your skies when you least expect it, reminding you that even after the heaviest rains, there's always a spectrum of hope.

And who knows, maybe one day, I'll tell you tales spun from swinging on the very rainbows we dreamt of seeing. Until then, keep your eyes peeled for the unexpected bursts of color in your life.

But, oh, this isn't a farewell; it's a 'see you in the next chapter.' Imagine me, a storyteller with a few more wrinkles and a heart rich with experiences.
Will yellow still be my beacon, casting a warm glow on the next two decades? Will sunsets continue to orchestrate a dance within my soul or will the moon whisper new tales?? I'm curious, as you might be, about the genre that will spill from my pen. Perhaps it'll be a journal, a guide, a novel or a mosaic of life's kaleidoscope—only time will unveil that chapter.

With hopes, dreams, and the promise of future adventures,

Furled.

Hush! You've come a long way, and I'm giving you a virtual pat. Now, treat yourself to your favorite dish. Pen down your experiences, thoughts, and reviews in the next page :

Once you're done, send it to furlywrites@gmail.com.

www.ingramcontent.com/pod-product-compliance
Lightning Source LLC
LaVergne TN
LVHW061607070526
838199LV00078B/7204